GOD HELP ME!

These PEOPLE Are DRIVING ME NUTS!

Other Crossroad Books by Gregory K. Popcak, Ph.D.

God Help Me! This Stress Driving Me Nuts!
Finding Balance Through God's Grace

Holy Sex!
A Catholic Guide to Toe-Curling, Mind-Blowing, Infallible Loving

A Marriage Made for Heaven
The Secrets of Heavenly Couplehood
A Marriage Enrichment Experience for the Parish and Small Groups
Leader Guide with DVD, Couples Guide

GOD HELP ME!

These PEOPLE Are DRIVING ME NUTS!

Making Peace with Difficult People

Gregory K. Popcak, PhD

A Crossroad Book
The Crossroad Publishing Company
New York

The Crossroad Publishing Company
www.CrossroadPublishing.com

Library of Congress Cataloging-in-Publication Data

Popcak, Gregory K.

God Help Me! These people are driving me nuts : making peace with difficult people / Popcak, Gregory K.

p. cm.

ISBN 978-0-8245-2597-2

1. Christian life—Catholic authors. 2. Interpersonal relations—Religious—Catholic Church. I. Title.

BX2350 .P58

248.4'82—dc21 00-067842

CIP

Printed in Canada

Contents

Acknowledgments

Just as a baby comes into the world with the help of a great many loving, competent hands, a book's birth is attended by many such people who hold the author's hand through the sometimes difficult process of labor and transition.

First among those people are my wife and children, who serve, each in their own way, as editor, critic, sounding board, reality check, delight, anchor, and friend. I thank God for their love, prayers, and support, without which I would not want to get out of bed each morning, much less do the work I do.

Likewise, a warm word of thanks to Mike "six-degrees-of" Aquilina, who, acting as erstwhile agent, connected me with Loyola Press in the first place. In my humble estimation, Mike should be a saint, save for the small technicality that he is still living—and may it be a long life. (Incidentally, Mike, I know you are getting weary of my perpetually acknowledging you in my books, but you're just going to have to get over it.)

I wish also to express my gratitude to the folks at Loyola Press for their fine work on the earlier edition of this book. Jim Manney, for his interest and fine judgment in choosing to publish this book in the first place. Vinita Wright, for her ability to be this book's midwife and bring it to birth. And Heidi Hill, whose intelligent questions and fine editing helped me communicate what I really meant to say! Thank you as well to The Crossroad Publishing Company for their work and creativity in preparing this second edition.

I also wish to thank God for giving me something to say (although, sadly, not the wisdom to know when to shut up) and BVM, my second mom, without whose kind prayers neither I nor this book would be.

Finally, I thank you, dear reader, for letting me into your life in some small way. I pray that you will find me to be good company on this part of your journey.

1

Aaaaarrrrrrrrrggggg!

I love Christianity. It's Christians I hate.

~ G. K. Chesterton

Some days it seems as if they are everywhere—people who are intent on making our lives miserable. Try as we might, we can't escape them. Our spouse is driving us crazy, our kids are plotting a coup, the boss is just plain insane, and the neighbors? Don't even get us started.

While this is true even in the best of times, when times are tough, it seems impossible to tolerate others. We're just trying to pay the mortgage, keep a roof over our heads, and keep the kitchen filled with our daily bread. But when our hearts are squeezed by worry, our minds are spinning with pressing troubles, and our strength is failing us, even basic civility can seem like a mission impossible.

The answers to such problems would be easy (say, a poisoned apple? or at least a poisoned pen) if only we didn't like to think of ourselves as civilized or moral. Christian Scripture tells us, "Love your enemies, do good to those who persecute you." Like it or not, every delicious revenge fantasy we otherwise well-meaning citizens conjure up is automatically spoiled by that nagging bit of Spirit-pricked conscience. "If someone slaps you, offer them the other cheek as well."

But how are we supposed to turn the other cheek when a coterie of our closest friends, not to mention society at large, is screaming names at us like "sucker!" "victim!" "enabler!" or the dreaded "codependent!" for even thinking of such a thing? And to be perfectly frank, look where the best practitioners of this doctrine—Gandhi, Martin Luther King Jr., Jesus Christ—ended up. Our spirits are as enthralled by such shining examples of moral courage as our flesh is repulsed at the thought of suffering the slightest discomfort or the smallest indignity, let alone dying for our faith. Gandhi once commented, "Everybody is eager to garland my photos, but nobody wants to follow my advice." And Jesus chided his disciples in the Garden of Gethsemane, "Could you not stay awake with me even one hour?"

Let the Buyer Beware

And yet, if you've picked up this book, you want to live on that more noble level. You're looking for healthy solutions, and you want to find the balance between doormat and dictator. If you abide by a Christian worldview, as I do, you understand that yes, we must encounter irritating, obnoxious, controlling, demeaning, exasperating, and otherwise grating people in our lives, but we must respond to those individuals differently from how the world in general is inclined to respond to them. Jesus tells us that "even pagans" love those who love them in return, but Christians are obliged to do more. We must respond to difficult situations and difficult people with a white-knuckled dedication to the virtues of faith, hope, and love.

Now, before I get too "het up," as they say in the mountains not too far from my office, perhaps I should mention that I will not be setting myself up as any kind of model for you to follow in these pages. When my wife mentioned to her sister that I was offered a contract to write a book on making peace with difficult people, my dear sister-in-law, who knows that I have a nasty habit of going on at some length about people who irritate me, noted dryly, "Oh! I didn't know he could write a book like that."

Touché. So, exactly what does qualify me to write a book like this? Several factors, the first of which is that I have had more than my share of practice in putting to work the techniques presented in these pages. Likewise, wherever possible, and however painful it may be, I will happily share some of those experiences with you. But even more important than my own experiences are the stories of the many faithful men and women I have been blessed to know. Thanks to my work as a counselor and as the director of the Pastoral Solutions Institute, an organization that offers seminars and telephone counseling for Catholics struggling to apply their faith to marriage, family, and personal problems, I am daily a witness to the efforts of countless people who fight against their baser instincts to do what

God and their consciences command while (and here is the real trick) not becoming a doormat in the process. The fact is, God may call some of us to become martyrs, but he* has little use for doormats, and it is important to know the difference.

In a later chapter, I will discuss the differences between living an ethic of self-donative (supremely generous, attentive, vulnerable) Christian love and being a doormat. But now I want to introduce you to some of the people who have been helped by the techniques presented in this book. Whether or not you find yourself identifying with any of their stories, I hope that they will encourage you to believe that there is hope for you in your unique circumstances. In this book, you will discover many of the secrets of making peace with the people who make your world a more difficult place to live in.

Bill at Work

When I met Bill, he was an account representative at an advertising firm. His abrasive manager, Eric, had what Bill considered to be an offensive sense of humor and expected Bill to cancel family obligations at a moment's notice to handle even minor issues that arose at work.

For the most part, Bill was able to cope with these issues. It wasn't easy, but Bill was good at his job and was respected by his coworkers. This made the tension Bill felt in Eric's presence bearable. One day, however, Bill decided that he had to draw the line.

Eric had been working with Bill to land a new account. They were to take their new client out for dinner, and Eric insisted that the best place would be a local "gentleman's club." While Bill knew that the client probably would not mind being taken to such a place, Bill objected to the idea on several levels. In addition to having the obvious religious and moral objections, he felt that taking a client to a strip club was unprofessional and degraded both the client and Bill's company. He and Eric got into a heated discussion, during which Bill insisted that if the meeting was held at a strip club, he would not go.

---

* Throughout this book, male pronouns will be used at times in reference to God. This is for ease of reading and is not meant to identify God as male in gender.

Eric was livid. He accused Bill of being a Holy Roller who thought he was better than everyone else. Bill kept his cool and did not back down. Finally, Eric agreed to hold the meeting elsewhere, but not before telling Bill that if they lost the account it would cost Bill his job.

Fortunately, Bill did manage to land the client, but Eric continued to harass Bill. He consistently gave Bill the less profitable accounts to manage, and Bill had the entirely justifiable sense that he was being not so subtly pushed out of the company. Bill was at his wit's end when he made an appointment to see me. "I'm not sure if I should quit or how to handle the situation, but I know I can't go on like this."

Using some of the strategies that I will present in this book, Bill was able to go over Eric's head to resolve the problem in a respectful and efficient manner. Bill had been uncertain how the company vice president, Eric's boss, would react to Bill's complaint, but we were able to design a respectful, non-threatening way for Bill to press his case. As a result, the vice president began making quiet inquiries into Eric's dealings with other employees, all of whose stories supported Bill's position. Within two weeks of Bill's bringing the matter to the vice president's attention, Eric was sent to "sensitivity training" by the human resources department and was warned that if his workplace behavior did not improve, he would be terminated.

While Eric continued to make things mildly unpleasant for Bill, the situation improved dramatically. Likewise, Bill's deft approach to the problem earned him the respect of the vice president, who told Bill that he would like to see him in upper management. Shortly after we concluded our sessions, Bill called me to say that he had indeed been promoted to a position similar to Eric's, but in another department. He rarely had to deal with Eric now, and he was looking forward to the increased salary and control over his schedule.

Not every workplace problem can be resolved so serendipitously, but you will be able to use the methods we discuss to make the best out of even the most difficult office situations. And these methods apply to marriage and family problems as well.

Anna and Larry

Anna and Larry had been married for fifteen years when they contacted me. While they had always had difficulties when it came to arguing, lately it seemed that the situation was getting worse. They fought over and over about the same issues and never arrived at any resolutions. Worse still, their arguments were causing deep and bitter resentments, with Anna feeling more and more that Larry was "controlling" while Larry characterized Anna as "never satisfied." "I can't do anything to please her," Larry said.

They had seen a notice about the Pastoral Solutions Institute in a Catholic magazine and had called me to arrange for telephone counseling, because finding a counselor who would be respectful of their faith journey was important to them.

After I gathered some background information, we were able to get right to the core of the matter. We discussed the patterns their arguments followed and compared these patterns to the arguing styles of couples who fall into a group I call "the exceptional 7 percent." I discuss these remarkable couples (15 percent of all married couples, 7 percent of married couples in their first marriage) in my books *For Better…Forever!* and *The Exceptional Seven Percent: Nine Secrets of the World's Happiest Couples.* The couples who are among the exceptional 7 percent exhibit much greater levels of fulfillment, satisfaction, and longevity in their relationship than more "average" couples do. This is due to many factors, not the least of which is their ability to feel closer to each other *because* of their arguments rather than *in spite* of them.

Over the next few weeks, I was able to pinpoint the skills both Larry and Anna needed to practice in order to experience their arguments as opportunities for greater intimacy and partnership rather than as competitive verbal-boxing matches that left them exhausted and resentful.

After four sessions, Anna and Larry were beginning to experience a major shift in the way they felt toward each other. While they were still suspicious about the permanence of the change, they had begun to resolve some of their most difficult issues—such as financial and sexual conflicts—with little loss of temper. As Anna told me, "I didn't really believe you when you said that we could feel closer to each other *because* of our arguments—especially considering our history—but last night I experienced it for myself. We helped each other stay focused, we were able to continue being loving to each other even at the hardest point of our talking, and we actually came up with some answers that I think we are both very happy with. Most of all, I felt like Larry respected me and really listened the whole time, and I tried to do the same for him."

After a few more sessions, during which we concentrated on shoring up and maintaining the changes, Larry and Anna told me that they had never felt closer. In our final phone session, Larry told me, "Two months ago, I was pretty sure this was going to end in divorce, but you'd never know it now. I don't think I've ever felt so loving toward Anna, and I don't remember the last time I felt this loved by her. The things we learned in these meetings have really made a huge difference."

In the next few chapters, we will review some of the techniques I taught Larry and Anna. But the techniques presented in these chapters don't just work for couples; they can also help parents negotiate even the toughest parenting problems.

The Collier Family

When Linda called me, she was in tears. The police had just brought home her fifteen-year-old son, Mike, who had run away from home a week earlier when his parents had grounded him for skipping school. Apparently, he had been keeping out of sight during the day and staying in a friend's garage at night. His parents had reported him missing, and the police had picked him up when they saw him wandering the streets during school hours.

Linda and her husband, Peter, were unable to get Mike to come to counseling, so they came without him to find out what they could do. We discussed many options, even the possibility of having the courts declare him incorrigible and having them commit him to an adolescent treatment program, but I discouraged Linda and Peter from exploring this option until we could try some less restrictive measures.

Because Mike was both resistant to the idea of therapy and basically uncommunicative, especially toward his parents, it was difficult to determine the intentions behind his defiant behavior. Instead, we had to focus our sessions on setting clear expectations, consequences, and parameters so that his parents could help Mike learn to behave more responsibly. If that didn't work, they could then place him in an environment in which he could be taught to behave more responsibly.

We concentrated our efforts on attempting to present Mike with choices that would require him to behave more responsibly. We were able to come up with a plan that Linda and Peter felt might work. They explained to their son that if he no longer wanted to live with them, he could choose to attend the adolescent treatment program. If, on the other hand, he did not want to go there, he would have to consent to three things: first, he would have to attend school faithfully; second, he would have to become involved in either school activities or volunteer work, or both; and third, he would have to attend counseling with his parents.

Of course, Mike was hostile to these suggestions. He accused his parents of trying to control his life, but his parents remained firm. "We told him that we wanted him to live with us, but more important, he had to get control of his life. He could either start doing it with our help or he could go someplace that would require him do it without our help, but that was entirely his choice."

The next few months were a very difficult time for the family. The complete breakdown in rapport between Mike and his parents made limit setting next to impossible at first. Linda and Peter had to concentrate not only on getting Mike to adhere to their rules but also on winning his heart back. In fact, if they were going to succeed, they would have to do this first.

Linda and Peter worked with me to find ways to reach their son. After several false starts, it was Peter who first broke through Mike's defenses. "I was going out to work on the car," Peter told me in session. "I always ask him to come and help, but he usually begs off for one reason or another. This time he agreed to join me. I was thrilled, but I tried to play it cool so I didn't scare him off. We worked quietly for most of the afternoon changing the brakes and listening to his favorite music."

When they were done, Peter took Mike to an empty parking lot. "His sixteenth birthday is coming up in a month, and so I gave him a short driving lesson. He knows that he can't get his license until he is doing better at home and school, but I think he appreciated the time together. He was a lot more respectful to both his mother and me that day and even after."

Peter and Linda were able to capitalize on this rapport in several other instances even as they continued to enforce clear limits with Mike. Finally, Mike agreed to come to therapy with his parents. Cautious at first, he warmed up as the weeks went by. With Mike's help, we were able to use several of the techniques presented in this book to move things along more efficiently. By the end of the school year, Mike's situation was greatly improved. He was maintaining a solid C average (up from a D) and was involved in several school activities. And he began attending the parish youth group. While he was by no means a perfect child, Linda and Peter felt that they had their son back. As Linda said, "I know he's getting ready to grow up and leave, but it's nice to think that it might happen on good terms and that we could help him get some direction in his life."

Parenting is a tough job, even when your children aren't difficult, but some of the techniques in this book can make it a bit easier by helping you maintain good rapport with your children as well as set and enforce appropriate limits.

Lastly, I want to introduce you to Connie and Jared. Their story will show you how, even if your life and problems seem as convoluted as a soap opera, the techniques presented throughout *God Help Me! These People Are Driving Me Nuts* can empower you to find peace in the face of some very difficult circumstances.

Connie and Jared

Connie and Jared had been married for twelve years when Connie came to see me. The year before, they had gone through an especially difficult time in their marriage. At the time, it had seemed certain that they would divorce. Jared had even moved out for a few weeks. Even so, through counseling, they had been able to put their relationship back together, and in the last year, Connie and Jared had both said that they felt more in love than ever.

The problem was that Connie had just found out that during the previous year, Jared and Connie's best friend, Morgan, had had an intimate relationship that was all but sexual. During that time, Jared and Morgan had met regularly, commiserated, kissed once or twice, and even declared their love for one another. Jared had broken off the emotional affair within the first weeks of his and Connie's marriage counseling. But Morgan, who was also having marital problems, was not so willing to give up on the relationship. Though Jared kept her at a distance, Morgan continued to insinuate herself into the couple's life for the next year, and she looked for every opportunity to reestablish the intimate friendship she had once had with

Jared—all the while fostering her friendship with Connie in an attempt to stay close to Connie's husband.

Jared had not told Connie what had transpired between him and Morgan, mainly because, as he put it, "I'm a coward." He explained that he was embarrassed by the relationship and that when things had started going well between Connie and him, he didn't want to bring up an issue that, as far as he was concerned, was resolved. Likewise, when it was clear that Morgan wasn't going to go away, he was afraid to hurt Connie by telling her how two-faced her "best friend" really was. It was a poor choice, of course, but he thought he could handle it himself. For the most part, he had managed to keep things quiet until one night when Connie and Jared went to a party at which Morgan and her husband were also present. Morgan had had too much to drink and began flirting with Jared out in the open. When he spurned her advances, Morgan began screaming at both Jared and Connie. She accused him of leading her on and told Connie all the details—plus a few embellishments—of her and Jared's relationship the year before.

As you might imagine, Connie felt horribly betrayed. It took several weeks before she and Jared could stabilize their relationship. And this was possible only because Connie and Jared had built up rapport over the year since their counseling. When Morgan saw that her attempt to split up Connie and Jared had failed, she became more vicious. She began spreading rumors about Connie. She threatened to turn Jared in to his professional board, because he was an attorney and some of their tête-à-têtes had occurred in his office. Likewise, Morgan began gossiping about Connie and Jared in the community. This brings us to the reason Connie came to see me.

Connie, Jared, Morgan, and her husband were all active members of the same parish, and Connie and Morgan served together on several community boards. Circumstances constantly forced Connie to be civil to a woman who would just as soon see her dead. Connie told me, "When I go to church, I see her there and I want to kill her. I haven't been to communion in a month because I can't think of anything else when I'm at Mass. I tried to go to a different parish last week, but the whole time all I could think about was that I'm not about to let that bitch drive me out of my church. I know that's not the attitude I'm supposed to have, but I can't stop myself from thinking that way. As if that wasn't bad enough, I have to see her when I take my son to baseball and my daughter to school. And she is so fake in public. She is all smiles and polite talk when she sees me, but she tries to stab me in the back every chance she gets. I end up looking like the idiot because the best I can seem to manage in public is ignoring her. Everybody wants to know why I'm being so cold to her. They seem to forget that she was trying to sleep with my husband and ruin me at the same time! How am I supposed to get on with my life when everywhere I go I see *her* staring at me with that big, fake smile?"

How, indeed. It may surprise you to know that Connie was able to find peace in this situation. By using the techniques and attitudes I will describe throughout this book, she was able to forgive Morgan for her deceit. And though they will never again be friends, Connie can be in Morgan's presence without wanting to kill her. As Connie put it, "I'm finally at the place where I can be around her and feel all right. Even though she is still less than kind to me, I understand that there is nothing she can do to hurt me. I am safe. My husband loves me. My life is good. I find myself praying that God will give her the peace he has given me in my life. I never thought I'd do that. I figured it would be good enough if I stopped praying that she would be hit by a bus. Thank God I've really come a long way."

It took a lot of work for Connie to get to that place, but she was able to do it because it was important to her to be the kind of person that God wanted her to be in this situation. She could have easily run from the problem. She could have dropped out of community service, changed parishes, enrolled her daughter in another school, and signed up her son for another team. But she struggled until she found the grace she needed to challenge her own pettiness and pride. And she became a better person in the process.

A Map and a Light

Whether or not you were able to identify with the people you just read about, their stories illustrate the fact that, given the right tools, you can bring about effective change even in the most difficult people and situations in your life. One thing all of these individuals had in common when I first met them is that they had almost given up hope. Connie was ready to pack up what little was left of her life and hide under a rock. Bill was ready to quit his job and maybe even bail out of a career into which he had invested many years. Anna and Larry were ready to give up on each other. And Peter and

Linda were certain that they had lost their son. And yet, in a relatively short period of time, they not only resolved the problems they were facing but also were able to bring about changes that made their lives better than ever.

Perhaps you believe that your situation is hopeless. Maybe you think you will never learn to get out of your own way, or overcome that habit, or have the strength to resolve that long-standing struggle with yourself. Perhaps you are ready to write off your spouse as an intractable idiot and your marriage as unsalvageable. Maybe you have a child who is making you lose sleep every night, or a boss who haunts your dreams, or a neighbor who seems dead-set on making your life as unpleasant as possible. If you do, I want you to know that there is hope. Scripture tells us that we can accomplish all things through Christ who strengthens us. And this book will give you the tools you need to actualize that promise, because the information presented in these pages, more than just a set of techniques, will provide you with a means to a more effective way of life—and a powerful change of heart.

As you meditate on the lessons in this book, you will begin to be more forgiving of yourself and you will be empowered to see others with what I like to call a God's-eye view. That is, you will be able to look at the difficult people in your life, see through all their defenses, and understand what needs to be done to bring about respectful change. You will be able to set appropriate limits and you will discover how to encourage yourself and others to grow in faith, health, and fulfillment. You will be more forgiving of failures (be they your own or others') and you will develop a greater sense of understanding and empathy for those people you used to fear, dislike, or look down upon.

This sounds like an ambitious project, and it is. But it is important that you understand that I am not proposing my own philosophy of life here. Jesus Christ set the parameters. He is the one who tells us that we are to love our neighbors as we love ourselves, implying that both are essential for the Christian walk. He is the one who in one place tells us to "turn the other cheek" and in another tells us to "shake the dust from our feet" and leave to their own devices those who will not follow the path of righteousness. He is the one who cautions us against seeing the speck in our neighbor's eye while ignoring the beam in our own. He is the one who tells us that whatever we do to the least of his brothers and sisters, we do to him. This book is nothing more and nothing less than my attempt to offer some answers to the question "Exactly how do we do all that?"

The Bible, it seems, is not so much a how-to book as a what-to book. It tells us what we must become, but it does not spell out, with perhaps a few notable exceptions (such as fasting, praying, and fortitude), the hows of accomplishing that mission. For the hows we must turn to what Catholic philosophers have traditionally referred to as the "Book of Nature."

Catholics have historically looked to two "books": the book of God's word, which is the Bible, and the metaphorical book of nature, which is the study of God's creation. If the book of God's word is the way God the Son (Jesus Christ) reveals himself to us, then the book of nature is the way God the Father reveals himself to us. Everywhere we look, the Father's fingerprints are all over creation. By seriously studying creation through all the sciences, we read this book of nature, which reveals how God intended human beings and their world to work together. Moreover, these two books are completely compatible because God is the Author of all truth. The Father doesn't teach one truth while the Son teaches another. The Bible and the book of nature reveal *what* we are to become and *how* we are to accomplish that goal.

In this way, the theologian and the scientist serve complementary functions. Like the relationship between an architect and a building contractor, the theologian draws the plans and the social scientist figures out how, exactly, to erect the structure. Both the theologian and the scientist are subject to the same divine authority.

In the same way, psychology, when wedded to Christian theology, is a powerful tool that can help us discover how to accomplish all those lofty goals Jesus Christ sets before us. This book represents my attempt to illustrate how cutting-edge advances in counseling psychology can help you experience greater personal fulfillment and build the kind of supportive, uplifting, respectful, challenging Christian relationships that God is calling us to have—be that with our spouse, our kids, our employer, our neighbors, or others with whom we interact on a regular basis.

When the lessons I describe throughout this book began taking hold in my life, I noticed an immediate and surprising change. For almost all of my life, I had been a faithful, practicing Catholic who had enjoyed a personal relationship with God. I had been raised in the charismatic renewal and took the Life in the Spirit seminar before my first confession. Likewise, I had served in various parish ministries growing up, loved Mass, and had attended Catholic schools all the way through college. But there I was in graduate school, thinking, "*This* is what it means to be a Christian." Up until that point, I had never really understood what God saw in "those (obnoxious, disagreeable) people." Or, for that matter, what he really saw in me. After all, I have been known to be obnoxious and disagreeable—and on more than one occasion! I accepted that God loved me and that he loved those who came across my path, but I never really understood *how*. How could he, as the phrase goes, love the sinner while hating the sin?

In turn, I struggled to understand how, as a counselor—much less as a human being—I was going to encounter people who did all sorts of horrible things and reach out to them in love. After all, I had a hard enough time loving myself in spite of my own shortcomings. But as I applied to my spiritual life the things I was learning, it seemed as if all at once things became clear to me. I could see myself as God saw me. I understood how to love others in a way that was accepting and yet could still insist that they work to become the people God had created them to be. I could be loving to others and still be able to set and respect the kinds of boundaries that enabled my relationships to be healthy, encouraging, and reciprocal, instead of draining, discouraging, and one-sided.

Granted, understanding how to do all of those things did not guarantee my ability to live them out perfectly. I still struggle to practice these lessons every day of my life. But the difference is this: Where once I struggled in darkness, I now struggle with a map and a light to guide me. I still occasionally trip, get distracted, and take odd detours (and like most men, I still hate to ask directions), but now I can find my way back more quickly. I not only know where I am going—I have a map that tells me how to get there. And this is what I am offering you in *God Help Me! These People Are Driving Me Nuts*—a map and a light to help you find the footprints the Lord left behind on the path he first walked, the path on which each one of us is invited to follow him.

Looking down the Road

As we prepare to make our journey, I'd like to take a moment to give you a sneak peek at some of the landmarks we'll pass along the way. The first step to making peace with difficult people is understanding what our responsibility to love others really entails. Jesus said, "Anyone who says he loves God but hates his neighbor is a liar." Clearly, living an ethic of love in our life and relationships is one of the most important missions for Christians. But what does it mean to love? Are we required to have warm fuzzy thoughts about everyone we meet? Does loving require us to ignore the truly hurtful actions of others or always give in to another's demands—regardless of how unreasonable he or she might be? And what is the difference between Christian love and pathological martyrdom (codependence) anyway? We'll look at these questions and discover the meaning of true Christian love along the way.

Then I'll expose the secrets of loving the sinner while hating the sin. You will learn to see yourself and others with a God's-eye view. You will develop a mind-set that enables you to acknowledge very real flaws while not giving in to being judgmental, full of despair, dismissive, or self-righteous. To this end, you'll discover the secret to uncovering the positive intention or need that drives a person's sinful, self-destructive, or obnoxious habit/behavior. For example, the person with a compulsive habit (gambling, drinking, sex) may be looking for a way to find relief from the pain and stress of his life. The suicidal person may believe she has found the ideal "solution" to her problems. The child who throws tantrums may not know a more effective way to get his needs met. The incessant gossip may be looking for a way to feel accepted. The teen who is endlessly being grounded might actually be looking for a way to spend time with his parents (or avoid more serious peer temptations) while still looking cool to his friends. And so on.

Once you can understand the positive intention or need that underlies a problem behavior (your own or someone else's), you can then develop a plan for changing that behavior, using the five-step P-E-A-C-E process. Or, when changing the behavior is not possible, you will learn how to set firm but respectful limits that will allow you to maintain your dignity and emotional safety as well as your credibility in the eyes of others.

Next, I will give you many examples of how to fine-tune these techniques as you apply them to yourself—in your marriage, with your children, at work, and in the community at large.

All in all, I am offering a fairly thorough look at how you can foster wisdom and peace in your relationships with yourself, with others, and with God who made you. That said, I have three questions for you.

- Have you ever wondered what it would take to resolve those conflicts that sap your strength, undermine your dignity, and alienate the very people you ought to be able to draw strength from?
- Do you wish that you could overcome the despair that inhibits your self-esteem, serves as an obstacle to your social or career success, or poisons your relationship with your spouse, your children, or God?
- Would you like to discover the secrets to fostering greater peace and love in your life?

If you answered yes to any of these, then I invite you to turn the page. Let the change begin!

Your Mission, Should You Choose to Accept It: How to Love as Jesus Loved

[A certain kind of person] knows affection takes liberties. He is taking liberties. Therefore (he concludes) he is being affectionate.

~ C. S. Lewis
From The Four Loves

Let's begin with some situations that you may recognize.

Melinda became tearful as she described her marriage. She explained that everyone thought that Charles, her husband, was the greatest guy. And it was true. He was very gregarious in public, he frequently led the charge for a worthy cause, and he took time to listen to a friend's or a client's problems. He was the life of the party and was well regarded by most people he knew. But as Melinda joked, he remained a mystery—a person whom everyone liked but no ne knew. He never let anyone get close enough—especially his wife.

At home, Charles was either passively neglectful or outright abusive to his wife and four children. He was a workaholic and a serious social drinker who would often come home "buzzed" or even drunk after a late night with the guys from the office. His drinking made his already short temper hair-trigger, and as the years went by, he became more and more difficult to please, finding fault with almost everything Melinda and the children did. When Melinda would ask him to stop drinking or to spend more time with the family, he would explode. The reason she was crying in session was that the last time they had argued, he had struck her, the first time things had ever crossed the line to physical violence. I tried to talk to her about her need to attend to her own and her children's safety, or to at least find ways to pressure Charles to come to counseling with her, but she was reluctant to take any steps that would seriously address the problem. "I love him. And I know he loves me. He's just not very good at showing his feelings. No, he's just under a lot of stress from work and I need to learn how to respond to him better so that I don't add to his stress, I guess. I get a lot of peace from prayer, though. I figure if Jesus suffered so much because he loves me, I can put up with my husband's temper. It isn't that much to ask, I don't think."

Eric was a twenty-eight-year-old man who lived at home with his parents. He had been having difficulty finding work, especially since he had lost his license after not paying several speeding tickets. Eric was hopelessly irresponsible. He had lost several jobs due to unnecessary absences. He had dropped out of college. He rarely cleaned his room—that was his mother's job—and he treated his father as if he was an always-full bank account. When his parents would challenge him to find regular work, he would protest that he was trying to build a business and that they needed to give him time. His "business" consisted of occasional DJ gigs at local bars. Often he would be paid in drinks or, on occasion, with some cash under the table. It never amounted to much, certainly not enough to get his own place and pay his own way, but he was adamant that this was the only work he was willing to do.

Eric's parents consulted me to see what they could do to help their son. The problem was that they shot down each idea I presented. When I suggested that they tell him that he would have to either go back to school or begin paying rent, they objected that it was "too pushy." When I recommended that they at least insist that he help out around the house by washing his own clothes and cleaning his own room, they said, "He would never do that." When I suggested that it was within their power to require that Eric take on such responsibilities, they simply said that they feared driving him out. "If we ask too much of him, he'll just leave, and he'll never make it out there."

I responded that this might be exactly what Eric needed. He could either show responsibility at home or learn it the hard way on his own. His parents looked at me as if I just didn't get it. "We could never do that. We love him too much. How is that a Christian thing to do? Wouldn't Jesus want us to be patient with him?"

Just What *Would* Jesus Do?

Love is a difficult thing to do well.

Historically, Christians have wrestled with finding the balance between two perspectives of Jesus. On the one hand, we know the Jesus who courted no one's favor and encouraged his disciples to shake the dust from their feet if a town would not hear the truth of the gospel. On the other hand, we also recall the Jesus who would "empty himself and become a slave," "suffer for our iniquities," and heal us by his own wounds. Christians sometimes find it difficult to sort out the difference between codependency and true Christian love because the church places such a high premium on sacrifice and self-giving. In such an atmosphere, it becomes all too easy to justify an unhealthy tolerance for the abusive, irresponsible, obnoxious behavior of others. For alums of the Christians-as-codependents school, the logic goes, "We are Christians. Therefore, we must willingly tolerate every kind of offense a person chooses to heap upon us. After all, didn't Jesus suffer for our sake? Who are we to not take up our cross and follow him?"

As with every good lie, there is a grain of truth in the above philosophy. As Christians, it is our privilege to have been given the graces that empower us to sacrifice ourselves for the good of others, to join, as Paul writes in Colossians, our sufferings with Christ's for the good of the whole church. There is a way to do this that is helpful, and there is a way to do this that is destructive to ourselves and to those we are trying to help. The case studies you just read depict the unhealthy Christian-as-codependent method, because these individuals believed that their status as Christians forbade them from ever putting their foot down to protect their own God-given dignity. But yet another school of thought is equally as unhealthy as the first—though for different reasons. I call this second group the "Jesus wants me to be happy" school.

Jack wanted to leave his wife. He had no significant justification for this. He was simply tired. True, he and his wife had a history of unresolved arguments between them, but this could have been resolved easily with some basic training in communication and problem-solving skills. When I shared this opinion with Jack, however, he was unmoved. "I think that when two people really love each other, it shouldn't be so hard. I've always heard that Jesus suffered so that we wouldn't have to. I don't agree with those Christians who think that life is all about suffering and being miserable. Life is too short, y'know? I think that Jesus wants me to be happy, and I know I would be a lot happier if I was out of this marriage."

The couple was insistent. Their fourteen-year-old son, Andrew, was incorrigible. The last straw, the most recent incident in a long line of behavioral problems, had happened only days before our first appointment, when he was expelled from junior high for bringing a knife to school. How could he be so irresponsible? his parents wanted to know. They made my role clear. It was my job as his counselor to "fix him." If I was unsuccessful in my attempt— and they were almost certain I would be—they would have him removed from their home and sent to a juvenile treatment center for long-term care. "God knows we have tried," said his mother, "but at this point, I don't think even God would blame us for thinking of sending Andrew away."

At first, I assumed theirs was the justifiable frustration of parents who had suffered too long, endured too much. But as we talked, it became clear that something else was at work.

As Andrew's parents related his history, it became painfully obvious what was wrong. One of the best definitions of *spoiling* I have ever read is "the combination of overindulgence and neglect." If this is true, then Andrew was a poster child for the spoiled. Both of Andrew's parents were very motivated to be the best at their work. Long hours at the office, business travel, and more long hours in front of the laptop were not unusual. And, of course, they had community involvements and church committee meetings—and Andrew had extracurricular activities, when he wasn't dropping out of them. While they said they loved their son very much—and I did not doubt their sincerity—the amount of time and emotional energy they invested in Andrew did not reflect that love. True, he led a very privileged life. He had the right clothes, the right sports equipment, and the right house in the right neighborhood, and all of these guaranteed that he would be allowed to hang out with the right kids, but he never had his parents.

> When he was a baby, a live-in nanny raised him. Then he attended daylong, year-round preschool. Then he went to school and summer-long camps. Now, it would be my turn. As his parents talked, it became apparent that unless Andrew was causing some kind of trouble, they barely acknowledged his existence. When his parents repeated their threat to send him away to a long-term program if he didn't shape up, I couldn't help but think to myself that they were abandoning their role before they had even started it. But as far as his parents were concerned, their position was completely justifiable according to their understanding of Christianity. After all, "God would understand." Wouldn't he?

If the problem with the Christians-as-codependents is that they never know when to stop sacrificing themselves for the sake of love, the problem with the Jesus-wants-me-to-be-happy adherents is that they often stop sacrificing too soon or never even get started. Individuals in this second group live in fear of being taken advantage of, perhaps because they have seen too many codependent Christians. Unfortunately, the Jesus-wants-me-to-be-happy philosophy does not withstand scrutiny. The Gospels say nothing of Jesus' desire for our earthly happiness. Would I agree that as a loving Father, God would rather us be happy than unhappy? Of course. As Scripture says, "If you ask him for bread, will he give you a stone?" and "Do not concern yourself with questions of what will we eat, what will we drink... Consider the lilies of the field. They neither toil nor spin, yet even Solomon was not arrayed as these!"

God is a generous God who longs to share everything (and then some) with his children, just as an earthly father would want to with his children. But membership in the divine kingdom has its privileges as well as its responsibilities. We cannot call ourselves Christians and simply enjoy the blessings while we ignore the responsibilities God gives each one of us. It is our ministry, our struggle, our cross, and our privilege to love into wholeness those he has put in our paths.

Was Jesus Codependent?

So how do we find a balance between responding to the call to love and setting healthy limits and boundaries with people? To answer that question, we need to take a closer look at Jesus' life and ministry.

The people in the two opposing schools we just discussed tend to look at only one side of Jesus' personality, ignoring the other important part. People from the Christians-as-codependents school have a particular devotion to the suffering Christ, the Jesus of the passion and the cross, while people from the Jesus-wants-me-to-be-happy school meditate more readily on the Christ of the resurrection and on the supernatural events preceding and following Pentecost. While these are important ways that Jesus reveals himself to us, they must be taken together; otherwise, we get an incomplete—and unhealthy—model to follow.

For example, if you meditate only on the resurrected Christ, you get the impression that Christianity is about looking for the happy ending. You get a theology that claims, "Yes, of course, there was all that suffering before, but now suffering is vanquished and we can all live happily ever after, drunk on the joy of Pentecost, which enables us to magically float over the problems and problematic people in life."

Would that it were so. Such individuals would do well to remember two things. First, Christ's victory was not gained *in spite* of the suffering that he endured, but rather *because* of it. And second, most of the apostles who were present at the Resurrection, the Ascension, and Pentecost also suffered a great deal after these events; in most cases, they met death in much the same manner as their teacher did.

Facing head on both difficult times and difficult people is an important part of living the Christian life. Christ's suffering does not excuse us from suffering; it merely gives our suffering meaning. After all, Scripture does not say, "Death, where are you now?" It says, "Death, where is your sting?" We still suffer, we still endure the barbs and indignities of others, we still die, but the meaninglessness, the humiliation, the sting is gone. "*Blessed* are those who suffer… "

If you're a member of the Christians-as-codependents school, on the other hand, and you concentrate only on the suffering and passion of Christ, it is likely that you will get the mistaken impression that Jesus was the most codependent person who ever lived—at least in the way that many people understand the term. Most people think that "codependent" refers to "any person who does for someone else something that he or she really doesn't want to do." Looking at it this way, it is easy to see why some people think that they must embrace codependency as a Christian way of life. "Jesus gave up his life for me. He certainly didn't want to ('Father, let this cup pass ...'), and I certainly didn't deserve it, but he did it anyway. In the same way, I must give my entire life to loving the most undeserving people I can find, whether I want to or not. My personal happiness or fulfillment is not the point. The only thing that matters is embracing the suffering."

Well, that certainly sounds very pious, but it is patently incorrect. Nothing in Scripture suggests that Jesus suffered just for the sake of suffering. When he chose suffering, either during his life (for example, through fasting or in dealing patiently with the ignorance of his followers) or in his passion, it was because he knew that there was no other way to meet the end goal—our reconciliation with God. In other words, Jesus understood the purpose of his life, and he was committed to fulfilling that purpose no matter what it took. Sometimes that meant subjecting himself to the abuse of others. Sometimes, though, it meant escaping the abuse of others, as when he avoided the traps of the religious leaders or escaped from those crowds who wanted to, alternatively, kill him or make him king.

While Jesus offers himself completely to those who will respond to him, to those who will offer themselves in exchange for all he has to offer them, he does not spend himself unwisely on those who cannot, or will not, reciprocate. To put it in scriptural terms, he does not cast pearls before swine. Jesus endured indignity, suffering, and humiliation *only* when doing so was absolutely necessary to fulfilling his mission, and then he did it with grace and fortitude. By contrast, the true codependent suffers because she or he has nothing better to do. She has no idea why she was created and has no sense of her greater purpose in life. As a result, she is unable to distinguish between necessary suffering, which results from efforts to become or help someone become the person God intended, and unnecessary suffering, which perpetuates a person's pathology or sin and destroys the person who is trying to help. Since the codependent is unable to tell the difference between these two kinds of suffering, she passively accepts all indignities and abuse as her lot. And for extra bonus points, and to ease the pain and conceal the absurdity of her circumstances, she overspiritualizes the whole experience, taking what would otherwise be nothing more than a big ball of pathology on legs and dressing it up in the costume of Christian martyrdom. "Yes, I am the victim of so much abuse and humiliation in my life, but isn't it wonderful? It makes me just like Jesus!"

Can We Really Demonstrate Christian Love?

By combining the images of the suffering Christ with those of the resurrected Christ, it becomes possible to see what Christian love really entails. It requires doing whatever is necessary and reasonable to help you, and the people you love, fulfill the mission all people were put on earth to fulfill.

Though the word *love* is popularly equated with things like feeling, passion, obligation, or duty, *love* is traditionally understood by the church to mean "the decision to will and work for the good of another." Granted, people strive for many "goods." Financial security, peace and quiet, entertainment, meaningful work, and a place in society are all examples of these. Of course, for the Christian, the ultimate good is becoming the person God created you to be. We are called to pursue this good in ourselves and in others over and above all the other lesser "goods" I already mentioned.

Applying this idea to relationships means that you can honestly say that you love someone if—and only if—you sincerely want that person to become everything God created him or her to be and you are willing to do whatever is within your power to make that happen. Let's take a look at each of these points.

How do you know what God created you, or someone else, to become? This is a tricky question, because too often we would rather make people in our own image and likeness than have them made in God's.

Tina was a lifelong Catholic who had recently had a "reversion" experience. That is, she had rediscovered the relevance of her faith after a long period of spiritual neglect. She regularly attended Mass and the adult education that her parish offered. She was also on the perpetual adoration schedule at her church and made time to say a daily rosary.

Much to Tina's disappointment, her husband, Harry, was not nearly as enthusiastic about the spiritual life. This became just one more thing to tax their already strained marriage. In counseling, Tina openly expressed her frustration and anger at Harry. "He is so stubborn!" She went on to criticize just about everything he did: the way he did not clean things to her specifications (not orderly enough), the way he spoke to their children (not firm enough), the way he related to her (not romantic enough), and the way he approached work (not ambitious enough). All this, in addition to the fact that he definitely was not spiritual enough. Harry, for his part, sat quietly with a pained expression on his face, looking as if he had heard all this before. She ended her litany by saying, "When I tell him all this, he accuses me of picking on him. I'm really not. I just want him to be everything he can be! But he never listens."

Aaron is extremely efficient and productive. A friendly yet no-nonsense person, he prides himself on his ability to juggle several projects at once and to manage his resources well, skills that make him much admired at work and enable him to accomplish more than what most people would consider an average amount of work.

His wife, Wendy, is much more laid-back. More nurturing than task-oriented, she enjoys spending time with their three small children—reading to them and cuddling with them as well as negotiating and supervising their play. She is a likable person, but not exactly what one would call a go-getter.

Aaron told me in session that he sees it as his husbandly duty to help his wife become the person God created her to be. As far as Aaron is concerned, this means that he must "make" her become more disciplined and organized. He makes schedules and job lists for her to follow, and he becomes angry with her when she either refuses to follow them or simply ignores them. He feels frustrated, "betrayed," and annoyed, which results in serious arguments between them during which Wendy accuses him of being "controlling" and he accuses her of being "passive-aggressive, lazy, and a bad Christian [for her lack of discipline and self-sacrifice]."

As well intentioned as both Tina and Aaron may be, truth be told, they are seeking to make their spouse more in their own image and likeness than in God's. Granted, there is nothing wrong with becoming more spiritual, or more disciplined, or more organized, or more appropriately self-sacrificing, but Tina's and Aaron's approaches leave something to be desired.

To will another person's good does not mean that you force that person to become just like you. It means that you are willing to listen to her, that you actively inquire about what she needs, wants, and desires from life. It means that you ask pertinent questions when she talks about the things that interest her and that you show an appropriate degree of interest yourself. It means that when she talks about something you are not interested in, you do not push her off on her other friends but you learn to acquire a taste for that interest. This doesn't mean that you have to be as crazy about widgets or doohickeys or the American Society of Humdingers as she is, but it does mean that if you care about her, you will not be dismissive of such things and you will work—for the sake of love—to develop at least the ability to ask intelligent questions about the subject.

In other words, if you really are interested in helping a person become what God created him to be, your first step should be to *ask him* who he thinks that is, and then you should be quiet and listen. For example, if you wanted to know what it would mean to work for my good, you might ask me what I would need to feel more fulfilled in my life, what kinds of activities bring me joy, and what areas I struggle with and feel that God is calling me to look at. Such questions will not only elicit what I already think, but they also will challenge me to look inward, to discover the daily-evolving plan that God has written on my heart. Ecclesiastes says, "Follow the vision of your heart, the path of your eyes." Not only do such questions challenge me to consult the vision that God has written on my heart, but they also clarify the path before my eyes, a path that can often be obscured by the stress that accompanies the effort to simply make it through the day.

It is important to keep in mind that you are helping me discover my path; you are not discovering it for me. Likewise, if you see an area of weakness or struggle in my life, you should resist the urge to jump in and fix me unless or until you secure an invitation to do so. The rule of thumb when helping others is wait to be invited to the party before you offer to bring the potato salad. You might say, "Greg, I notice that you have a really hard time keeping on top of everything. I'm pretty good at organizing things—would you like some tips?" If I say yes, then (and only then) may you suggest some ways I could lighten my load or offer to help me yourself, all the while resisting the urge to do it for me or to become frustrated with me if I don't take your advice quickly enough. Whether or not I take your advice (or accept it in the first place), we will grow closer if you use this approach, because I will see that you not only care enough to lend a hand, but you also care enough to stand patiently by while I struggle to reach that hand.

In short, the first step to living true Christian love is taking the time to listen. In my counseling practice, I confront all sorts of problems. It would be easy for me to start yelling at the people who come to me with these issues. "What's wrong with you? What are you doing? Can't you see how destructive this is?" But this approach would be as useless to me professionally as it would be to you personally. To do such a thing may make me feel good—it may allow me to think, "Well, I really told him, didn't I? Good for me for standing up for the truth!"—but it won't help me help the person or address the problem. All it does is alienate the person I am talking to. He still has the problem, but now he will keep it a secret from me. I get to think, "Problem solved," and he simply learns not to trust me anymore.

Instead, I have learned to confront other people's problems not with my own agenda in mind, but with the agenda God has written on their heart. After I have listened for a while to a person describing his or her struggle, I will say, "Tell me a little bit about the qualities you wish to be known for at the end of your life." Initially, most people are confused by the question, so I press a bit further. "In other words, do you want to be known as a loving person, a strong person, a disciplined person, a person with a good sense of humor, a principled person? How do you want people to describe you after you are gone?"

Once I get a short list of the qualities that are especially important to the person, I ask a second question: "If you were to live out those qualities (lovingness, creativity, discipline, patience, understanding, wisdom, peace, etc.) in this situation, how would you behave differently from how you do now?"

The effect is dramatic. Though sometimes my clients are loathe to admit it, the answers to their problems suddenly snap into focus. Granted, it still takes time to make those solutions a reality, but they at least they have a map to follow, a map drawn not by me, but by the hand of God on their heart.

You can use the process I just described to bring about change in two ways. First, you can use it to clarify your responses to other people. Second, you can use it to respectfully challenge others to change. Complete the following exercise.

SEEKING THE GOOD FOR YOURSELF AND OTHERS: AN EXERCISE

It is best to do this exercise with someone close to you, like your spouse or a close friend. Later we will discuss other methods you can use with people who are not so close to you.

Seeking the Good for Yourself

Prayerfully consider the qualities you most *wish to be known for at the end of your life.* Be specific (for example, loving, wise, understanding, strong). List the most important of these qualities on a sheet of paper. Ask your spouse or close friend to do the same.

Think of a situation that causes you to act or feel toward each other in a way you don't like (for example, you lose your temper when arguing with your spouse or you become irritated with a coworker). Write that situation down.

If you were to apply the qualities you listed in the first part of the exercise to this situation, how would you behave differently from how you do now? Be specific. For example: What might you say differently, when might you say it, what tone of voice would you use? Generally speaking, would you be more patient? more forceful? more loving? How would you act if you *were* more loving (confident, forceful, patient, understanding) in this problem situation? Speak only for yourself. That is, talk about what you need to do differently to be more consistent with your own spiritual ideals. You must not (at this stage of the game at least) tell you partner what he or she is doing incorrectly. Write your thoughts down and share your answers.

Make a commitment to help your spouse or your friend be more faithful to his or her desired qualities both in the situation he or she just mentioned and in daily life. Do so in the following way: When you see your partner or friend acting in a manner that seems to be inconsistent with his or her stated spiritual ideals, respectfully and gently say, "You told me that you would like to be more (fill in blank) in your life. Help me understand how what you are doing (or what you are saying, or how you are behaving) helps you become that kind of person."

The final step in this exercise is a very respectful way to challenge your spouse or friend to stay true to the qualities he or she would like to possess. No one likes to be challenged, but doing it this way gives a person little room to be defensive—if she is really serious about living out her faith. While other exercises in this book will help you deal with people with whom you do not have such a strong rapport, we begin with the people closest to you because they are sometimes the hardest people to challenge respectfully. Remember, the key to working for your own or others' good is discovering the kind of person you want to be at the end of your life and supporting each other as you struggle to become that person.

MaryBeth and Allison had been friends since childhood. Sadly, Allison was going through a difficult period in her life and was desperately seeking answers to some very hard questions. A troubled relationship combined with job stress had lately made Allison more and more irritable. It had also made her very confused as to what her next steps should be in her job, in her marriage, and in her life.

MaryBeth was at a loss. Her friend kept coming to her for support, but nothing MaryBeth said helped. The last time they were together, the situation had reached critical mass. MaryBeth had delivered her usual pep talk about how she was sure that God had his hand in Allison's life and that everything would work out for the good of those who love him, "just like Romans 8 promises," when Allison erupted. "What do you know about it? I'm really tired of everybody throwing platitudes at me. I pray, and I talk, and I think, and nothing gets any better. I just get more and more confused. Everything is NOT all right, and I really resent you pretending that I can just think happy thoughts and make it all go away."

MaryBeth called me at the Pastoral Solutions Institute to ask how she might be able to better support her friend. We discussed the previous exercise and how it might be helpful in her situation. Although she was initially skeptical, she agreed to give it a try and to call me the next week for a follow-up session.

In our subsequent phone conversation, MaryBeth was pleased to say that some progress had indeed been made. "It helped in two ways," she said. "First of all, it helped me figure out how I needed to approach Allison. On my list of qualities, I wrote that I needed to be more sensitive, more understanding, and a better listener. I figured out that Allison really didn't need me to try to put a happy face on the situation for her; she just needed a friend she could talk to and who would stand by her while she struggled."

MaryBeth explained that after they had patched things up, she suggested the exercise to Allison, who was desperate enough to give anything a try. They talked about the qualities Allison would need in order to feel more in control when trying to solve her problems at home and in the office. She said that she wished she could be more confident, patient, and strong. Then Allison thought about how she would act differently in her problem situations if she were to practice those qualities. If she were stronger at work, for example, she would respectfully tell her boss what she was really thinking instead of hold her hurt inside when he criticized her. At home, she had been begging her husband to go to marriage counseling with her. Now, if she possessed the qualities of strength, confidence, and patience, she would insist that they go and would tell him that even if he wasn't willing to go, she was going to start without him.

As the weeks went by, MaryBeth told me that whenever she and Allison would meet, Allison would tell MaryBeth about her struggles to live up to the goals she had set for herself. For her part, MaryBeth would just keep bringing Allison back to the qualities that were important to her. When Allison complained that her boss had criticized her unfairly again, MaryBeth was able to ask if Allison had respectfully stood up for herself. Often she did, but in those times when she didn't, MaryBeth was able to ask Allison, "But how did keeping it all inside help you become the strong person you said God wants you to be?" When Allison wanted to cancel her first counseling appointment because her husband was still refusing to come with her, MaryBeth just said, "Of course I'll support you in whatever you decide, but how would canceling your appointment help you become stronger or more confident? You said you wanted to be patient. Don't you think it would be better to go to the appointment, be patient, and see if Art [Allison's husband] doesn't come around in a few weeks?"

Allison didn't always like hearing these things, but she respected MaryBeth for helping her and for being a true friend. Several months later, MaryBeth called to give me an update. Even though Allison's boss was still a difficult person to deal with, she felt much more confident standing up to him, and when she saw that there were no repercussions for her newfound assertiveness, she was able to take her boss's negative comments—which had decreased significantly—with a grain of salt. Likewise, Art had started counseling with Allison the week before. Though they had a long way to go to repair their marriage, Allison felt confident that they could at least begin to work together. And she and MaryBeth were closer than ever, because MaryBeth was the only person who really understood the kind of person Allison wanted to become and who could support her in that struggle.

Seeking the Good for Others

The second part of true Christian love is helping another person fulfill the vision of the person God intends him or her to be. But before you can do that you must learn what it means to will the good of another person.

In order to work effectively for another's good—the way Christians ought to do it—we must understand what we can and cannot reasonably be expected to do. As I've already suggested, Christians must be willing to make remarkable sacrifices when fulfilling our mission requires us to do so, but we are not expected to spend ourselves just for the sake of spending ourselves. The Jesus who gave himself over to his Roman executioners for the sake of our salvation is the same Jesus who refused to chase after the rich young man who would not sell all he had, give the money to the poor, and follow Jesus. Jesus offers all of himself to those who are willing to respond, and although he never writes off anyone, neither does he go chasing after people when they are not ready to be pursued.

In the same way, working for another's good means knowing when to give and when to hold back. This is one of the major questions I deal with every day in my own work as a counselor—not to mention in my life as a human being. When facing problematic people, it is important for me to know when working for their good requires me to actively assist them and when it requires me to hold back. So how do I learn this? Basically I need to know two things.

- Can I offer my assistance to this person or attend to his or her problem without causing my primary obligations (my family, the ministry/work God has given me) to suffer unduly?

- Is this person asking me to work harder than he or she is willing to work to solve his or her own problems?

God has entrusted to me certain people (my wife and children) for whose spiritual growth, physical well-being, and emotional health I am directly responsible. Likewise, God has given me a specific job to do (my work/ministry) so that I can fulfill my part in helping to establish God's ways on earth. I am primarily responsible before God to do these two roles well. Whatever energy, time, and resources I have left after attending to these two God-given assignments I should offer to other people and other ministries. The same is true for you.

So if a problem situation or a problematic person has a direct impact on my family life or on my work, then I am obliged before God to do whatever is in my power to help that person or resolve that problem, because it affects the areas over which God has given me primary charge, and if I don't attend to that matter, no one else will. In the same way, if a problem situation or a problematic person does not directly affect my family or my primary work/ministry and I can offer my assistance *without causing an undue burden to my family or my work/ministry,* I am still obliged to help.

On the other hand, if helping the person or resolving the problem requires my family or my work/ministry to suffer undue hardship—with regard to the time or any other resources I provide them—then my Christian duty *requires me* to distance myself from that person or problem. Such an attitude is critical for my preventing an overcommitment to nonessential work or my avoiding overinvolvment with certain people who have a talent for occupying all my time—that is, those who are either too chaotic or too entertaining to leave alone.

Adopting the above strategy keeps us humble, because it reinforces the idea that you and I are not personally responsible for the well-being of the entire world. That is God's job. We are only responsible for fulfilling the roles and ministries God has given us. To spend ourselves on ministries that are not our own or on people for whom God has not given us primary responsibility—at the expense of our primary responsibilities—is nothing more than escapism. We all know people who spend every spare minute on extra work, community involvements, or church service while ignoring their family and the responsibilities God has given them. We all know people at the workplace who not only do the work God has given them to do but look for other work/ministries that they can do, not to fulfill God's plan for their life but to make themselves shine in the eyes of others. These people are simply running from the primary ministries God has given them. This is not Christian service, but some form of cowardice, escapism, pride, or self-aggrandizement. We would do well to avoid it.

Neither is it reasonable or within our Christian obligations to work harder at solving another person's problems than he or she is willing to work at it. Look at Jesus' own example. He does not die on the cross so that we don't have to. He dies on the cross and then tells us to take up ours as well. He is willing to work hard for our salvation—he is willing to fulfill the ministry he alone can fulfill—but he expects us to work just as hard. Scripture says, "Work out your salvation in fear and trembling." It does not say, "Slide into heaven on Jesus' coattails." He opened the door—as only he could—but he did not then pick us up and carry us over the threshold. That's why we were given feet.

Let me offer you a personal example. As a therapist, I work very hard on other people's problems all day long, and most of the time they work just as hard, if not harder. Every once in a while, though, I find myself being sucked into a client's problems and notice that the client is not doing anything to help him- or herself. On certain occasions—more in the earlier years of my practice than now—I have killed myself to offer suggestions and support to a person or a couple, even to the point of losing sleep thinking about how I could help them. And when they return to session the following week, they haven't followed up on any of my suggestions; they haven't come up with any of their own solutions; they have slept very well themselves, thank you very much; they didn't even bother to come up with any ideas regarding an agenda for our meeting; and they now expect me to exhaust myself again because, they say, "You're the therapist. That's your job."

You have probably had similar encounters with family members who wouldn't lift a finger to save their own lives but expected you to come to the rescue at the drop of a hat. Or with so-called friends who lived from chaotic moment to chaotic moment and expected you to be their anchor. Or with certain likeable but chronically irresponsible or self-destructive people whose charm made you feel guilty if you ever even thought about not cleaning up their messes for them. And if you ever complained about your predicament, your cries were probably met with some version of "Well, you're the parent/spouse/friend/teacher/boss. That's your job."

I'm not saying that you should become coldhearted; I'm just saying that you shouldn't work harder on other people's problems than they are already working or are willing to work on them. In order to gain your assistance, a person does not need to be making a perfect effort on his or her own behalf, but he or she must at least be making a sincere effort. And if she is making a sincere effort, it's right for us to stand by her as long as necessary. But in those times when she is unwilling to try as hard as she is able, sometimes the most loving thing we can do is leave her alone until she decides that she must take at least some responsibility for her own problems. The apostle Paul, who established churches and set up leadership within them in various cultures and climates, admonished that those who did not work should not eat. Paul was getting at the principle I'm describing here.

In a later chapter we will talk more about setting appropriate limits, but for now it is enough to know that sometimes working for another's good means giving all we have and sometimes it means holding back.

Crusaders, Go Home!

Understanding what Christian love does and does not require of us is an extremely important first lesson in learning how to deal with difficult people.

Of course, Christian love requires one more thing of us, and that is to keep our crusades to ourselves. I touched on this in the section on willing the good of another, but I'd like to develop the theme a bit more now. "We must keep our crusades to ourselves" is another way of saying that in dealing with difficult people, we must resist the urge to concentrate all of our energy on changing them. Rather, we must find a way to change ourselves so that we can better tackle the situation. As Scripture has it, "Do not see the speck in your neighbor's eye, while ignoring the beam in your own."

We all know this, but every single one of us still falls prey to the temptation to pour all of our energy into fixing other people when we should be changing ourselves to respond more appropriately to our circumstances. My schedule is clogged with husbands who want me to fix their wives, wives who want me to fix their husbands, parents who want me to fix their children, and people who want me to give them the secrets to changing the irritating people in their life. Most of these people are Christians of one stripe or another, and all of them know that the only person you can truly change is yourself. But that doesn't stop them from exhausting months and even years of energy on the useless goal of changing someone else.

I will present in this book a lot of techniques to help you effect change in others, but in order for these techniques to work, they have to change you first. When I was in fourth grade, my mother went through a time when she felt utterly abandoned by certain friends she had trusted and counted on since childhood. Matters were not helped by the fact that these were all religious people who used their position in the church group in which my parents served to ostracize my parents. My mother told me later that every day she would pray, "Lord, change them. Help them see what they are doing. Please, make them stop hurting me."

The only response God had for my mother was that she was praying the wrong prayer. That her prayer should not be "Lord, change them," but "Lord, change me." She resisted this message at first, but finally, in desperation, she began praying that second prayer. Only then did she begin to find peace. The Lord did change her. He made her stronger. He made her not need those individuals any longer, and years later he gave her the grace to see that those people's ministry did not bear good fruit and that she and my father were spared a greater pain in the long run. Even though she lost those friends in the process, she was given peace in return and the grace to see God's wisdom.

I need to give credit to my mom for teaching me her "Lord, change me" prayer early in life. More times than I can count, that prayer has helped me gain wisdom and understanding far beyond my years and capabilities. Sometimes when I would say it, the "Lord, change me" prayer caused me to accommodate myself to others. I became a better servant, a more patient friend, a better listener, a kinder husband, a more attentive father. Other times, it gave me the grace I needed to leave behind unhealthy relationships, commitments, and situations. Either way, it has always given me a great deal of peace.

As you read through *God Help Me! These People Are Driving Me Nuts* try to take the focus off the others in your life and bring your crusade home so that you might save your own soul and preserve your own peace of mind in the process. By understanding what Christian love really calls us to do (and not do) and by remembering that it is not your job to change other people (only yourself in response to those other people), you will be on your way to mastering the first lessons of making peace with difficult people.

3

Ac-cen-tu-ate the Positive: How to Discover the Motives behind the Behavior

To understand is to pardon.

~ MADAME DE STAËL

Why oh why do people act the way they do? Can't they see how crazy they're being? Don't they know that people are beginning to avoid them?

"Why" is the question. In fact, it's the first question we must ask when faced with difficult people.

"I'm telling you, if she doesn't knock it off, I'm going to lose my mind."

To help with expenses, Maria had taken in a roommate, and things were not going well. Chelsea, the roommate, tended to be very particular. She would argue with Maria about how much Maria's contribution to the utilities should be, how they should split the grocery bill, what the division of labor should be, and a million other niggling details. Likewise, she rarely did anything around the house unless it was specifically "her job" or "her turn" to do it. As if all this was not bad enough, Chelsea would often find fault with the way Maria cooked or cleaned, or even with the way she dressed. Comments like "You're not really going to eat that, are you?" "I thought you said you dusted," and "That's not your best look" were not unusual.

The last straw was when they hosted a combined Christmas party for their friends. The day of the party, Chelsea got stuck late at the office and left Maria to set up. Maria told me that this didn't bother her—people have to work, after all—but when Chelsea did arrive home, she didn't even express any gratitude. "All she did all night was point out how she would have done such and such differently and how sorry she was that she had to work late because if she had been around to help, things would have gone so much better. No one seemed to have a problem with the evening except her. I don't know who she thinks she is, but I'm here to tell you that I'm ready to toss little Miss Muffet right out on her tuffet if things don't change soon."

Paula, a telephone client, called me at the Institute to ask for help with her sixteen-year-old daughter, Rhea.

"Rhea shows me no respect at all. It's way beyond the normal teenage hate-your-parents thing. The really confusing thing about it is that sometimes she can be just as sweet as anything, but other times, all I have to do is look at her and she goes off."

Matters were not helped by the fact that Paula was not getting along with her husband, Cal, and that Rhea had recently begun inserting herself into the arguments between her mother and father, taking Cal's side.

"I need to find a way through this. It just breaks my heart because we used to be so close, but now I honestly can't stand to be around her, and she sure doesn't act like she wants anything to do with me."

In the last chapter, I suggested that the secret to creating change in others is to begin changing yourself. Now, most people groan audibly when I tell them this, because they think that I am going to ask them to do something unpleasant, like set themselves on fire or roll naked through an army of underfed ants or eat my cooking. No such luck.

The kind of change I am talking about is not unpleasant at all. In fact, it will actually make you a more optimistic, likeable, and empowered person. I am talking about a change in attitude.

You see, most of us really have no idea why people do the things they do. We experience people as being kind or mean, active or lazy, friendly or aloof, generous or cheap, pleasant or difficult, easygoing or demanding, and so on, and that's that. For simplicity's sake, we put people into nice, neat categories and then shun the categories of people we don't care to deal with. "He's a dishonest person." "She's a manipulative woman." "They're rude."

And yet, I suspect that not a single one of us would care to be dismissed so readily by someone else. I know from personal experience how much it bothers me when someone decides that I am a certain kind of person. Once someone has decided that, he or she has found an excuse to simply not deal with me anymore. Still, knowing how this feels has not always stopped me from doing it to other people. I imagine the same is, or has been, true for you. We forget the words of Jesus: "The measure you measured with will be measured back to you." This wise teacher warned us again and again that it was not our place to judge others, but to love them.

Admittedly, this is easier said than done, but when you are able to get beyond the labels, understand *why* a person does what he or she does, and appreciate those motivations, then not only is forgiveness possible—as the quote beginning this chapter suggests—but change is too. Of course, in order to understand others on a deeper level, you will need some tools. That is what this chapter is about: helping you to develop the skills you need to see through the obnoxious, irritating, and even self-destructive and sinful behaviors that you and other people engage in and to find opportunities to create understanding, forgiveness, and change.

Loving the Sinner While Hating the Sin

Cum dilectione hominum et odio vitiorum.
"Love the sinner, hate the sin."

~ ST. AUGUSTINE
From Letter 211

In essence, when I talk about the need to learn why people do what they do as the first step in creating change, I am really talking about learning how to love the sinner while hating the sin. This is one of the most well-known maxims of Christianity, and although most of us are familiar with the phrase, very few of us know how to put it into practice. It is much too easy to lapse into one of two alternatives. The first is the "hate the sin *and* the sinner" attitude that seems to serve as the basis for much of what passes for "conservative" politics these days. The second is the "love me, love my sin" attitude that tends to be espoused by Christians of a more liberal persuasion, who tend to mistake muddleheaded compassion for true Christian charity. But we are going to avoid these extremes and look for the golden mean, the truth between the two poles.

How exactly do we love the sinner while hating the sin? To answer that question, I need to give you a brief psychology lesson.

What's in It for Me?

The fields of medicine and psychology both refer to a phenomenon called secondary gain, which is the benefit a person gets by behaving in a less than healthy way. For example, imagine that I have the flu and you make a fuss over me. I might not like being sick, but I *do* like the attention I get (secondary gain), so I might be tempted to exaggerate my illness—or stretch it out a bit—to enjoy more of that attention (or time off from work, or something else that I enjoy). Secondary gain tempts us to act in an unhealthy way in order to achieve some benefit.

This concept does not apply only to malingerers and hypochondriacs. The same is true of people who have any obnoxious habit, attitude, or behavior. I, like most people, do not wake up in the morning thinking to myself, "How many ways can I irritate those closest to me today?" And yet, that is often the very thing I end up doing. Why? Because I am not paying attention to my irritating behavior; I am only thinking about the secondary gain, that is, how acting this way is going to help me achieve a goal—a goal that seems good to me. For example, let's say I treat you in a brusque way. Certainly my intention is not to be mean. I am probably just trying to hurry up and get to all the things I need to do (an objectively good goal), but in the process I end up treating you in a less than kind manner. Or, let's say I choose not to do my paperwork today. Am I trying to irritate my secretary or the insurance company? Of course not. All I am doing is desperately looking for a way to get five minutes of work-free peace (also an objectively good goal), but in the process I unintentionally end up making someone else's life a little bit harder. In both of these situations I intended to do something good (get my mind organized, find some peace and quiet), but I went about it in a bad way. My intentions were positive, but my methods were not.

Think about your own life. Remember those times when you just wanted someone to understand your point of view but you ended up hurting him or her in the process of explaining yourself? What about those times when you intended to act in a loving way but instead came off as needy and suffocating, or even callous and uncaring?

Before we go any further, take a moment to complete the following exercise.

WHAT'S IN IT FOR ME?: AN EXERCISE

This is an exercise in creativity. There are no right answers. Identify what your initial reaction would be in the following situations. Then list some possible benefits the person may be trying to gain by acting in an inappropriate manner. Finally, identify how you might feel or act differently if those were the true intentions behind the offensive behavior. Here's an example.

Situation: You are arguing with Alan. All of a sudden, he calls you a jerk.

Initial reaction: I want to say something hurtful in return.

Possible intentions: He didn't feel like I was trying to understand him. He wanted me to listen. Or he was trying to let me know that I hurt him in some way.

If these were the true intentions behind the behavior, how might you respond differently? Instead of getting defensive right away, I would ask him to explain himself better. I would probably try harder to understand his position instead of retaliating right away.

Situation: Your spouse forgets to do something very important that you had asked him or her to do.

Initial reaction:

Possible intentions:

If these were the true intentions behind the behavior, how might you respond differently?

Situation: You feel that your friend has been neglecting you lately and that you have been carrying the relationship.

Initial reaction:

Possible intentions:

If these were the true intentions behind the behavior, how might you respond differently?

Situation: At work, you are passed over for a job you thought you were guaranteed to get.

Initial reaction:

Possible intentions:

If these were the true intentions behind the behavior, how might you respond differently?

Situation: Your child is speaking to you disrespectfully.
Initial reaction:
Possible intentions:
If these were the true intentions behind the behavior, how might you respond differently?

Think of something you have done recently to which others have taken offense. Was it your intention to be offensive? What was your true intention? How might you go about meeting this intention more respectfully in the future?

I am not suggesting that just because we understand the intention behind the behavior we must automatically forgive every stupid and obnoxious thing that someone does to us. Rather, understanding is merely the starting point for respectful change. We cannot hope to create change in our relationships if people experience us as their adversaries. So to build the rapport needed for respectful change to happen, we must challenge our initial inclinations to lash out and instead seek understanding of the true intention behind another's offensive behavior. As St. Francis said, we must not so much seek to be understood as to understand.

Don't You Get It?

As you read Ralph's story below, you will see another example of how easy it is for a whole lifetime of intentions to be misunderstood and the sad consequences that can result.

Ralph had been married for thirty-five years when his wife left him. Ralph's grown children sided with their mother, virtually alienating Ralph from the family. As far as they were concerned, Ralph was a taskmaster as a parent, unaffectionate, a workaholic, and, frankly, a general pain in the ass who justified his abrasive—they might say verbally (though never physically) abusive—nature with pious religious practices and spiritual platitudes. When I talked to Ralph, though, he was completely nonplussed.

"I just don't understand. All I was trying to do all those years was provide for my family. They say I wasn't affectionate, that I pushed too hard, that I was critical. Well, I was trying to toughen them up so that they could live in the real world. I always told them, 'If I criticize you, that means I love you and I want you to be your best.' They say I was a workaholic. Well, how the hell else was I going to provide those college educations, that roof over their heads, those things and vacations they wanted? My wife never had to worry about a thing. She never had to pay a bill. I handled it all. Every single one of those kids grew up, stayed out of trouble, and learned how to make a living. I taught them that. I refuse to believe that I could have been that horrible of a parent. They might not agree with my methods, but they learned what I wanted them to learn. My old man raised me the same way, and I thank God he did, because I would be half the man I am today if it wasn't for him."

Truth be told, Ralph's methods did leave much to be desired. He was completely misguided about the best way to be a husband to his wife and to train his children to take their place in responsible society. In fact, many of the methods he chose—not affirming his children, not being present physically or emotionally, pushing everyone too hard, being too heavy-handed in marital decision making and parental discipline—were directly responsible for his children's delayed launching into the world (most of them had lived at home until their late twenties) and the ultimate deterioration of his marriage. Even so, Ralph wanted the same thing every parent wants: children who have what it takes to make it in the world, children who can fulfill their potential, exhibit self-discipline, be well-provided for, and have inner strength. Ralph's intentions were as good as any other spouse's or parent's intentions, but his approach was not effective.

Ralph's story is a good introduction to a concept promoted by certain psychotherapists, such as John Grinder and Richard Bandler, who assert that *every behavior*—even obnoxious, irritating, and self-destructive behavior—is the "attempt to meet a need or positive intention." The key to loving the sinner while hating the sin is learning to respect the intention behind the behavior, even while we reject the faulty way that the intention is being acted upon. We can reach out with love and support to Ralph, the sinner, with his good intentions, even while we wholeheartedly reject his faulty methodology, the sinful ways in which he expressed those God-given intentions.

Ralph, misguided as he may have been, is not a jerk, an ass, a demon, or any other name his family wanted to pin on him. He is a man who wanted good things for his wife and children but was clueless about how to effectively achieve those ends. He used what tools were available, and tragically, those choices cost him everything he held dear.

Does seeing Ralph in this light excuse him? No, it does not. Am I saying that his wife and children should now forgive him all his failings and welcome him back into the family with open arms? No, I am not. It is not as simple as that. Even though Ralph's intentions were good, his methods caused a lot of harm, and he is responsible before both God and his family for healing as much of that pain as possible. In all our meetings, I was very direct with Ralph about how his methods were truly flawed, but even when I was being most critical of him, he never felt rejected by me. Even in these sessions, he would say, "You really understand what I was trying to do. Even though it hurts my heart when I think about what you say, I know you're right. I appreciate your helping me through this."

Ralph could accept what I had to say because he felt I loved him, understood him, and supported the positive intentions behind his behavior, even though I openly condemned the way he expressed those intentions throughout the years. He could join me in hating his sin because he, himself, felt loved and supported.

Just What Do You Mean by "Sin"?

I'd like to take you a little deeper into this concept. To truly understand what it means to love the sinner while hating the sin, we should probably examine our terms a little more closely—especially those uncomfortable-sounding words *sinner* and *sin.*

I had originally intended to title this book *Loving the Sinner, Hating the Sin: Creating Change in Your Own Worst Enemy.* But my publisher suggested I find an alternative title, since confronting a buyer with the words *sin* and *hate* on the cover might turn people off. I didn't have a problem with the original title because I tend to think of sin in a very different way from the way most people do—although it is an entirely "Catholic" way of thinking about sin. But after some initial irritation, I had to agree with my publisher. People are put off by the words *sinner* and *sin* because they are words that call up images of evil people who engage in midnight orgies with demons in the back corners of dark, stench-filled alleys (insert spooky music here). And of course, none of us is anything like that.

And although sin often involves darkness and even "evil," at its root it is something else entirely. In essence, sin is accepting less than God wants to give you. God is generous, and he wants to give us all of himself. We don't deserve such a gift, we have no right to ask for it, but he wants to give it to us. Even so, we are reluctant to accept that gift, and this reluctance to accept God's perfecting presence is sin. For a million different reasons, we allow ourselves to be open to some of God's goodness while we reject the rest of it. Did you ever wonder how sin could "hurt" God, as the good sisters taught us in Catholic school? Sin hurts God because it offends his generosity and wounds our relationship with him in the process. The parable of the prodigal son is a good example of what I am talking about. In it, we not only find a parable of God's mercy, but we also discover the true definition of sin.

The parable is of a young man to whom the world belongs if only he can wait until he is mature enough to handle it. If he can just wait, surely his fortune can grow even greater, the family's influence and esteem can grow even wider, and his ability to nurture that fortune can grow as well. But he is full of himself. He wants it all, now. *Even if that means accepting less in the long run.* His father wants to give him the world, but this fool will settle for a bag of coins. And it only gets worse.

After the prodigal wastes his inheritance, he finds himself living with pigs. At any time, he can go back home, but he is proud. The same arrogance that caused him to demand too soon his share of the fortune blinds him to the history of generosity his father has shown him. As Jesus tells the story, there can be no mistaking that the father has never given his sons any reason to doubt that he would love them and accept them no matter what, for he is the personification of generosity. But the prodigal cannot see that. He has a mansion to go home to, but he would rather live with the pigs than overcome his pride!

This is what sin is: refusing our fortune, denying the generosity of our heavenly Father, and preferring to live among the pigs. Let's try another metaphor. Imagine that you are wealthy beyond your wildest dreams. Walking down the street one day, you see a man who is destitute. Something inside you cries out to help this person. More than that, you feel the grace of God calling you to change this man's life for the better, forever. You get his attention and you tell him that you want to give him a million dollars and a new home.

The man frowns. He tells you that even if he did believe you—and he doesn't—he is perfectly happy living the way he does, thank you very much, and he doesn't need the help of any rich do-gooders. No matter how much you insist, he refuses you. In fact, he becomes more and more hostile the harder you press. Finally, you have no choice but to leave him to his own company.

Wouldn't you be hurt? Why? Because your generosity was offended. That beggar represents each one of us. The beggar's choice represents sin. God wants to give us the best of everything: "Ask and you shall receive, seek and you shall find, knock and the door shall be opened unto you" and "If you ask for anything in my name, you will receive it."

But we will not have it. Through the next door is a treasure room filled with riches of love, fulfillment, providence, joy, community, strength, wisdom, and everything else God wants to give us, but we prefer to stay put. Seen in this light, sin is not so much something to be condemned as it is something to be mourned.

God teaches us that we can have both/and. Sin teaches that we must settle for either/or. It is sad when a man like Ralph believes that in order to raise children who can make it in the world he must withhold love and affection from them. It is sad when, rather than learning how to meet our own needs while still being respectful to the needs of others, we simply push ahead, blind to the cries of others. It is sad when, in an attempt to get you to listen to me, I act in a way that instead alienates you. This is even more tragic in light of the fact that God wants to teach us that we do not have to choose. We can expect the best from our children and be as affectionate as we can be. We can seek to be understood even while we practice understanding. We can have personal fulfillment *and* build a community of love and solidarity around us at the same time.

Understanding this is extremely important. Creating change in yourself and in others depends on your ability to see the positive intention behind offensive behavior and to help the person find an *even more efficient and productive way to meet that intention.* For example, Ralph believed that the only way he could prepare his children for the world was to withhold affection from them. But what if I could show Ralph a way to prepare his children to make it in the world and still be a loving, generous man? Do you think that Ralph would have preferred that? Of course he would have.

Similarly, I often see couples in counseling who argue viciously because they think that they must compete with each other to get the things they want out of life. But what if I could help that husband and wife discover a problem-solving method that would allow both of them to meet their needs? Do you think they would prefer that way? What about the suicidal man who thinks that the only way to solve his problems is to kill himself? What if I could show him a way to solve those problems and still have a long, happy life as well? Would he not be interested in that? In each of these cases, a positive intention is struggling to find a respectful way to express itself. By being able to help these individuals find more rewarding, efficient, and respectful ways to satisfy their intentions, I am able to help them leave behind their sinful, destructive, disrespectful ways and become more like the people God created them to be.

In the next chapter, I will show you how to create similar changes in yourself and in the people around you. But first I want to put this approach in the context of traditional Christian teaching.

Church Chat

Some people become concerned that this whole idea of there being a positive intention behind sinful behavior is somehow unchristian. After all, what about all that famous Catholic and Baptist guilt? What about our fascination with original sin?

Well, as a Catholic myself, I certainly would say that original sin is a reality, but Catholics are far from fascinated with it. In fact, the church teaches that because of the sacrament of baptism, we are freed from the bonds of original sin. The truth is that the Christian tradition offers strong support for the idea that a positive intention is behind even the most sinful, destructive, or disrespectful behavior.

In the Catholic training of my childhood, I learned a mouthful of a word: *concupiscence.* Simply put, concupiscence is a strong longing, and in Christian tradition, it is the longing for the mud that remains even after baptism washes away the stain of original sin. Perhaps another metaphor will help.

Imagine that you left your garden hose curled up every which way in the driveway. Moreover, imagine it takes you a while to put it away and before you do so you run over it with the car about a half-dozen times. When you get around to it, you find that the hose cleans up well enough and that you can straighten it out just fine, but as you attempt to coil it back up, it starts fighting you. Why? It's a simple matter of physics. The hose physically "remembers" the distorted shape it was forced to lie in for weeks, and it will continue to remember that distorted shape (and vex you) every time you try to roll or unroll it for many years to come.

In the same way, while baptism washes us clean and straightens us out—so to speak—our humanity retains the memory of the distorted thing it was before we were baptized (from the Fall to the Resurrection is a long time to lie in the driveway). Try as we might, when we aren't paying attention we have a tendency to want to return to this distorted shape. This is concupiscence—the tendency toward sin that remains even after the stain of original sin has been washed away.

Now, back to our original point—that a positive intention or God-given need underlies even the most irritating, destructive, or sinful behaviors.

The *Encyclopedia of Catholic Doctrine* defines *concupiscence* as "our tendency to choose a lesser good over a greater good." For example, everybody knows that promiscuity is a sin. But the reason it is a sin is not because it feels good, as some cynics suggest. Rather, it is a sin because the experience is objectively *less good* than working toward a vital, loving, respectful, mature, secure marital sexuality. No one in his or her right mind would argue that point. God wants us, his children, to have the best. And so he asks us to avoid those things that, although they may be superficially attractive, are decidedly lesser goods.

Likewise, the church teaches that concupiscence is not sinful in and of itself. It merely represents our tendency to be tempted into sin—choosing a lesser good over a greater good. A good scriptural example of this is Jesus' own temptation in the desert. Just look at one example of how Satan was trying to make Jesus sin. Satan promised that if Jesus submitted to him, he would permit Jesus to rule the world. To be perfectly honest, as far as I am concerned, the image of Jesus ruling the world is a pretty attractive one. A poverty-free world with comprehensive health care, environmentally friendly transportation, free all-you-can-eat seafood buffets at all participating Five Loaves and Two Fish restaurant locations...Nevertheless, this idea is decidedly less good than the salvation of every generation of humanity from the beginning of time. Jesus passed up a fairly decent proposition because it wasn't the best proposition. The best proposition, of course, was God's plan for Jesus' life, and that didn't include any kind of collusion with the devil.

To summarize, in order for anything else in this book to make sense to you, I need you to remember that very few of us actually wake up and say, "Ooh! I know! I think I'll see how many rotten, evil, offensive, sinful things I can do today. Won't that be fun?" More likely, when we do sin or act in an obnoxious, destructive, or offensive manner, it is because we do not know a better way to express our positive intention. I yell at you because I don't know a better way to get you to listen to and understand me. You can't overcome a certain bad habit because you can't think of a healthier, more respectful way to comfort yourself. Your neighbor picks arguments with people because he feels the need to prove that he is worthy of respect. And his neighbor cheats on her husband because she can't figure out how to meet her needs for intimacy and passion in her marriage. In each case, we would be right to take serious issue with the methods employed to meet these needs, but that does not give us the right to ignore the fact that an objectively respectable need or intention lies at the root of these behaviors.

In this chapter, I have attempted to explain why it is important to discover the intentions that lie at the heart of those behaviors we find offensive. Likewise, I have tried to show you how discovering these intentions is not only consistent with our Christianity but also an imperative part of living out our faith. In the next chapter, you'll learn how to discover the true intentions behind the hurtful actions of others and a five-step process for creating change.

4

Finding P-E-A-C-E When You're Going to Pieces: How to Make Change Happen

Peace, peace is what I seek, and public calm: Endless extinction of unhappy hates.

~ MATTHEW ARNOLD

Wanting to understand why people act as they do is merely the first step in dealing with the relationships that make us crazy. In this first step, we make a serious, personal commitment to seek the positive intention behind the offensive or hurtful actions of others. Next, we need to learn the skills that will help us discover these positive intentions. I use two major techniques in both my clinical practice and my personal life to discover the true intentions behind obnoxious behavior. The information I gain from these two techniques then becomes the basis for the five-step P-E-A-C-E process for creating change. I'll discuss this process later in the chapter. To get started, let's take a closer look at the two powerful tools you can use to uncover the true, positive intention behind an inappropriate behavior.

The Direct Approach—Just Ask

As the name implies, the direct approach is the simpler and preferred of the two methods. In effect, this method boils down to asking the person what he or she is trying to accomplish by behaving in such a way. This might sound like a no-brainer, but the ability to ask such a question does not come as naturally as you might think. When we encounter an offense, our normal reactions tend to look more like this:

"Why do you always have to act like such a jerk?"

"I can't count on you for anything, can I?"

"What do you think you're doing (you moron)?"

than like this:

"What are you hoping to gain by acting that way?"

"What reaction were you hoping to get out of me when you did/said that?"

"When you do/say that, I understand you to mean such and such, *but what are you really trying to tell me*?"

It takes practice to stand in the face of offensive behavior and not be offended. But you're going to have to do just that if you want to discover the positive intention or need that underlies a problem behavior. When someone acts in a hurtful way toward you—regardless of whether you think the action is intentional or not—you must resist the urge to criticize, accuse, become defensive, or attack. Instead of doing any of these things, you must take a breath and literally tell yourself that this person, being known to you as a basically decent individual (at least some of the time), probably did not wake up this morning thinking of new and creative ways to irritate you. Remind yourself that his or her offense is in fact the result of some miscommunicated positive intention and that therefore it is your job to respectfully find out what that intention may be, instead of merely reacting to the offensive behavior. So, instead of saying, "I can't believe you did/said that! You are such a pig!" or some other equally unproductive variation on the theme, you must ask a three-step clarifying question in which you 1) describe the offense, 2) state the effect the offense had on you, and 3) give the offender the benefit of the doubt. If you do this well, you will end up with a question that looks like this: "When you did such and such, I really felt hurt, but what were you *really* trying to do?"

In the first part of the question, simply describe the offense. Don't analyze it or interpret it; simply stick to the facts and describe it. For example, instead of saying, "You really acted like a jerk," which is your own analysis of the situation, simply say, "When you *looked at me that way* ..." or "When you *slammed the door* ..." or "When you *spoke to me in that tone of voice*..." In each of these examples, the italicized portion of the statement describes the facts of the event sans any opinions, condemnations, accusations, or interpretations. Saying it this way prevents a defensive reaction in the other person and increases the chances that you will be heard.

Part two of the question is where you respectfully offer what you understood the other person's statement/action to mean. To continue with our examples from above, you might say, "When you looked at me that way, *I really thought you were angry at me,*" or "When you slammed the door, *I thought you were upset that I asked for your help,*" or "When you spoke to me in that tone of voice, *I really felt humiliated.*" Again, you need to resist the urge to criticize, condemn, or accuse. Instead, you want to assume that a positive intention is behind this behavior so you will be content to simply describe the negative effect the behavior had on you—without any theatrics.

Having stated your interpretation of the event, you are obliged to let the other person know in the third part of the question that you are giving him or her the benefit of the doubt.

For example, instead of saying,

> "When you looked at me that way, I really thought you were angry with me, and that would be typical of you because you are impossible to please!"

you would say,

> "When you looked at me that way, I really thought you were angry with me, but what did you *really* mean by that?"

Or,

> "When you slammed the door, I thought you were upset that I asked for your help. Is that what you were trying to say?"

Or,

> "When you spoke to me in that tone of voice, I really felt humiliated, but I don't think that's really what you were trying to do.
> Is it?"

In other words, after you describe the behavior that offended you and what you took that behavior to mean, you need to ask the other person what he or she was really trying to communicate. This kind of question is great because it is a firm but gentle way of letting the other person know that he or she is coming across badly—whether it is intentional or not. At the same time, such a question doesn't give the other person anything to react to or become defensive about because the question is respectful. At all times, the person you're questioning sees that you are really working hard to understand where he or she is coming from.

More often than not, the direct approach outlined above works very well. Sometimes, though, you need a tool that is a little subtler. This is especially true when you are trying to identify the positive intention behind the behavior of a young child, an angry adolescent, or even an adult for whom self-awareness and personal reflection are not strong points. In such instances, you'll need to "follow the money."

The Indirect Approach—Follow the Money

When journalists Woodward and Bernstein were investigating the Watergate scandal, their informant told them to "follow the money" if they wanted to know the truth. You can use a similar method to discover the positive intentions or needs of those individuals who—for whatever reason—are less than forthcoming with you.

Following the money means looking for the obvious benefit a person gains from acting a certain way or, when such a benefit is not so obvious, looking at what happens *immediately after* the person exhibits that behavior.

Let's say, for example, that a child throws a tantrum. What is the benefit? If the parent caves in to the child's emotional display, then the benefit is obvious. The child is acting this way because he gets what he wants. But let's say that the parent isn't the sort of parent who gives in and the child throws a tantrum anyway. How can you discover the intention in this case? The best way is to look at what happens immediately after the child exhibits the behavior. Does the parent get angry? Perhaps the child is looking for a way to make the parent angry. Perhaps the child is angry with the parent and doesn't know a better way to express it (in which case the child needs to be taught more appropriate ways to express his anger). There are other possibilities as well. After the tantrum, does the parent leave the child alone? Perhaps the child is attempting to get some space and needs to be taught healthier ways to claim his independence. Does the behavior draw the parent closer to the child? Perhaps the child needs to be taught more appropriate ways to ask for the affection, time, or attention he wants.

Danny's case is a perfect example of discerning someone's intention by the indirect approach.

Danny was a six-year-old boy who was referred to the in-home family therapy program where I worked while I was a graduate intern. The most immediate issue was that Danny was throwing horribly violent tantrums that frightened his mother. On separate occasions, Danny had pulled a knife on his mother and had even kicked the family's television set, breaking it. One time, Danny threw a tantrum in front of me and my pregnant supervisor, threatening to "kick her tummy and kill the baby!"

Our first impression was that Danny wasn't getting enough attention from his single mom. The only problem with this hypothesis was that his mother was very affectionate. Each day when Danny would come home from school, she would spend a good deal of time telling him how much she loved him, looking at his work for the day, and talking with him about all the things he did. All in all, it seemed as if she was pretty clued in to her son.

We decided to back up and attempt to assess the intention behind the violent tantrums by asking, "When Danny throws a tantrum, what does his mom do differently from what she normally does?" What we discovered was that when Danny threw a tantrum, his mother would have to get off the couch and physically restrain him. This was no small feat for the woman, who was permanently disabled with chronic back problems. Not having much else to go on, we suggested that perhaps Danny was not getting enough physical affection from his mother, who, though loving, was much more verbally demonstrative than physically demonstrative of her affection—owing probably to her disability. We guessed that perhaps Danny's tantrums were actually a very clever adaptive response he had developed to meet his need for increased physical affection.

We explained our theory to his mother and offered the following suggestion. When Danny came home from school, she would continue their usual ritual of looking at his schoolwork and telling him that she loved him (visual and auditory attention). But from now on, she was to do this while he sat on her lap and she cuddled him, giving him physical affection for as long as he would stay.

Danny's mother took our advice and ran with it. Even though it made her physically uncomfortable, she held Danny, rubbed his back, stroked his head, and cuddled with him—sometimes for up to an hour—while she talked to him and reviewed his day. Amazingly, within a week, the tantrums had decreased significantly. Within a month, they were gone completely.

We were able to identify not only the positive intention behind Danny's behavior but also a dramatic solution simply by paying close attention to the immediate response to Danny's tantrums.

Another classic example of when to use this technique is when parents seem to have to ground their children constantly. I am regularly consulted by parents who complain that they have grounded their child for forever and a day, with no effect. Often the parents say, "It's almost as if he likes to be grounded." I usually agree that perhaps he does.

Especially for an adolescent, being grounded is a great way to either avoid trouble or spend more time with one's parents while still getting to look cool to one's peers. For example, one boy I counseled didn't want to go to a party his friends were having because there were going to be drugs there. But he couldn't say no to them because the peer pressure was too great. Instead, he broke curfew the night before the party, and his parents grounded him. He couldn't go to the party, yet he got to save face with his friends. Likewise, a fourteen-year-old girl I counseled was having a hard time coping with all the pressures of growing up. She wanted more time with her busy parents but felt ashamed that she needed them. As she put it, "I mean, it's not like I'm a baby or something." Her answer was to unconsciously do things for which her parents would ground her. It helped her avoid some of the issues she had with her peers, and it forced her parents to spend more time with her. In both of these cases, rather than continue to ground their child (and thereby reward the negative behavior), the parents concentrated on increasing the amount of time and affection they gave their child. They also taught their child that if he or she ever needed to use them as an excuse for avoiding dangerous situations, it would be okay with them.

The same strategy works with adults. Anna, a telephone client of mine, worked for a physician who loved to pitch fits. Anna and her coworkers would tremble when he found a mistake on a chart, and they would run around pell-mell trying to fix the error while he screamed at them. In counseling, Anna discerned that her boss's intention was to motivate his employees. Because the poor woman was at her wit's end, I helped her realize that she had nothing to lose by trying something different. After all, if things continued as they were, she would have to quit, but if she tried something different and it didn't work, maybe her boss would fire her, and at least then she could collect unemployment benefits while she looked for another position. She laughed about this and decided to try something that we talked about—giving her employer a healthier, more respectful way to motivate her.

The next time he started yelling at her, she ignored him and continued her work. He became angrier at first and then yelled, "Well? Didn't you hear what I said?" Anna replied, "I'm sorry, doctor, I was waiting for you to speak to me more respectfully. 'Please' usually works." I'll let Anna tell the rest of the story.

> *I was sure he was going to tell me to pack my things and get out. I was sick to my stomach while he was screaming, and I almost couldn't bring myself to say anything. But after I did, the room got deadly quiet. He just looked at me and then said in an exasperated—but much more respectful—tone, "Would you PLEASE find that patient's chart for me!?"*
>
> *I just smiled and said, "I'd be happy to, doctor," and he walked away shaking his head. I couldn't believe it.*

This was not the last time the good doctor lost his temper with his office staff, but it marked the last time Anna was afraid of it, and she and the doctor's relationship began to change. Eventually, she was promoted to office manager because of her continuing ability to deal effectively with even the most difficult patients who came in.

Would this same strategy work for everyone? No, but by looking for the positive intention in this particular situation, Anna was able to offer her employer a more efficient way to meet his intention. She was able to effect a positive change in her work environment—even without the willing cooperation of her boss.

Complete the following exercise to practice identifying the positive intention or need behind the offensive behavior of a person who is resistant to the direct approach.

FOLLOW THE MONEY: AN EXERCISE

1. *Identify a behavior that you find offensive.* Ideally, this behavior should be that of a person who will not talk with you about the problem or who lacks the maturity or insight to respond to the direct approach outlined earlier in the chapter. Write down the behavior.

2. *Identify, if you can, the obvious benefit that the person receives by acting this way.* Write down that benefit and **skip to item 4.** If you cannot identify the obvious benefit, go on to item 3.
3. *If you cannot identify an obvious benefit, then identify the immediate reaction of others after this person exhibits the offensive behavior.* For example, does the behavior cause other people to come closer, or does it cause them to give the offending person space? Is the behavior a way the offending person tries to motivate others to do things for him or her? Does the person use this behavior to force people to listen to his or her ideas? Is the behavior a way to get others to deal with issues they don't want to deal with? Is the offending behavior a way to express anger at someone who usually does not tolerate more direct expressions of anger? What other ideas do you have about the intentions behind this particular behavior? Write them down.
4. *Save your answer and use it in the five-step P-E-A-C-E process you will learn about in the next portion of this chapter.* For extra credit, you may begin thinking about other, more respectful ways the intention you listed in item 2 or item 3 could be met. For example, if a child is throwing tantrums to get something, how could you teach him more respectful ways to earn what he wants? If your spouse acts offensively because she doesn't believe you are listening to her, what things can you do to let her know that you are listening? Write down the respectful alternatives.

Welcome to the P-E-A-C-E Process

Now that you've learned two powerful ways to identify why people do what they do, it's time to introduce you to the P-E-A-C-E process, a five-step process for creating respectful change.

Practice working with, not against, each other.

Express your desire to help the other person meet his or her need or intention.

Assert more respectful and efficient ways to meet the need or intention.

Create a plan to help each other use these new, more respectful strategies.

Evaluate the results and make adjustments as needed.

Let's take a brief look at each of these five important steps.

Practice working with, not against, each other.

When two people have a conflict, they often treat each other as enemies. This is a mistake. One of the first things that happens when you begin making a conscious, consistent effort to seek the positive intention or need behind other people's offensive ways is that you stop viewing them as enemies. Instead, you begin to see them—in some cases for the first time—as people who struggle, just like you, to meet their needs, to find fulfillment, and to make their way through life as peacefully and as successfully as possible. And just like you, sometimes they make mistakes. To my mind, being able to think of others in this manner—especially others with whom we are in conflict—is the decisive factor in the litmus test of whether or not we are living up to Jesus' command to love our neighbors as ourselves.

Keeping this in mind, one rule of thumb applies to all conflict with other people. "The person is never the problem. The *problem* is the problem." It is not our job to attack, condemn, or dismiss anyone with whom we are in conflict. Rather, we must think of the other person as our *teammate* in solving the problem. The following is a good example of what can happen when we stop viewing others as enemies and begin thinking of them as partners in solving problems.

Jerry was having problems with his wife, Linda. He felt that she was very distant and argumentative, and their relationship was becoming more strained every day. He called me at the Pastoral Solutions Institute because he felt hopeless about his marriage and didn't know if he could do anything else to help himself or his relationship.

I asked him what he had done to try to fix the problem. He explained that he'd tried to talk to Linda directly about how unhappy he was with the way she was acting toward him and that she had refused to listen to him. In response to his complaints, she would become defensive, and the discussion would quickly go downhill.

On the surface, it seemed that Jerry had been very reasonable, but I suspected from his tone of voice that he approached his wife in a way that made her feel less like a partner and more like a criminal. I explained the idea of seeking the positive intention and asked him what his wife might be trying to do by acting in an offensive way toward him. After some thought, Jerry said that she often accused him of complaining and of being overly critical, and that maybe—although he couldn't be 100 percent sure—her being distant and defensive was her way of insulating herself from his alleged negativity.

I suggested that he approach her a little differently the next time and say, "Honey, I love you, but when you push me away like that, I feel really rejected. I know that's probably not what you're trying to do, but I'm having a hard time figuring out where you're coming from. Could you help me understand?"

Sure enough, by our next telephone session, Jerry had confirmed his initial suspicions. His wife did think of him as being negative and critical, and she distanced herself from him as a way of, as she put it, "not having to put up with the constant complaining." While Jerry did not like hearing what she had to say and still did not completely understand where she was coming from, he told me that it was the most productive discussion they had ever had about the problem. He also said that afterward, his wife agreed to join him in our telephone counseling meetings, "if that was okay."

Over the next several weeks, rather than simply accusing each other of wrongdoing and expecting each other to—in effect—"shape up or else," Jerry and Linda became much better at partnering with each other to solve their problems. By our final meeting, they had both said that they hadn't felt this good about each other in a long time and that they were confident in their ability to work together to respectfully resolve the problems that might come up in the future.

It is absolutely impossible to view as teammates those we used to think of as enemies unless we make a personal commitment to seek the positive intention or need behind offensive behavior. After all, why would I want as my teammate somebody I considered to be a "selfish SOB" or, in Jerry's case, a "neglectful, dispassionate spouse"? I wouldn't. But I *would* be willing to have as my teammate someone who I thought was a basically decent person and who cared something about me, even though he sometimes stuck his foot in his mouth or did thoughtless things (just like I do). And guess what? The difference between the "selfish jerk" and the "basically decent person" is all in my head. We will encounter very few, if any, sociopathic personalities who get their kicks by tormenting other people. Of course, you would never know this by talking to most of the couples I counsel, who are sure their spouse is out to get them (or, for that matter, by talking to someone after he has just been cut off in traffic). Some of these folks might lead you to believe that the world is full of people who have nothing better to do than intentionally work at making our lives less pleasant. But this is simply not the case.

As you become more skilled at seeking the positive intention or need that is hiding behind a problem behavior, you will see more and more how silly it is to view other people as enemies. You will be able to approach with love and respect even those with whom you have previously had the most difficulty. You will even be able to partner with these individuals to overcome the obstacles that stand between you.

Express your desire to help the other person meet his or her need or intention.

When we act in offensive ways, most of the time it is because we do not feel that the other person is on our side. We do not believe that the other person has our best interests at heart, and so we feel that we must choose between attacking them and not getting our needs met.

At the same time, the other person may be feeling the same thing about us. With this in mind, once you have taken the time to discover the positive intention behind a person's irritating behavior, you need to reassure her that you are willing to do whatever it takes to help her meet that need or intention, as long as she is willing to work with you to find more respectful ways to do it.

It might take some convincing to get the other person to believe that you are willing to help him meet his needs, especially if you and he have been at each other's throats for a while, but if you can manage this you will be doing two things.

First, you will be growing in your capacity to practice true Christian love. Recall from chapter 2 that love means being willing to work for the good of another. This is where that attitude comes into the problem-solving process. Now, instead of being dismissive toward those people you initially found offensive or off-putting, you will be partnering with them to help them find more respectful ways to express and meet their needs. You will in fact be loving them as Christ calls you to love them. And if you manage to grow in your capacity to express true Christian love, you will accomplish a second benefit. You will earn the respect and gratitude of someone you previously considered an adversary, and most likely, this person will be more willing than ever to partner with you to find more respectful, efficient ways to meet your needs.

Gina couldn't stand Merrill when Merrill first came to work for the company. Gina felt that Merrill was, as she put it, "a cold fish." Merrill was the only one in the department who kept her office door closed, and Gina felt she had a seemingly superior manner about her. In addition, Merrill had what some called an anal-retentive approach to record keeping. She was quickly on her way to becoming the least-liked person in the office.

While Gina's normal reaction would have been to put as much distance between herself and Merrill as possible, she decided that she would try a different approach this time. She invited Merrill to lunch one afternoon. And when Gina got an opportunity, she used the direct approach I outlined earlier in the chapter to ask Merrill what was motivating her aloof manner.

Merrill was initially upset to discover that her coworkers felt some hostility toward her, but Gina reassured her, saying that she had hoped that their lunch would be an opportunity for them to understand each other better and for Gina to discover if there was anything she could do to help.

Merrill explained that she understood where Gina was coming from, but that it really wasn't her intention to be difficult at all. The problem was that Merrill had always had a difficult time meeting new people. Even though she was quite confident about her work, she was fairly shy in social situations, and she suspected that her shyness was being conveyed as a superior attitude.

Over that lunch, Gina gained an ally in the office, and Merrill gained the help she needed to build better relationships with her coworkers.

In his famous book *How to Win Friends and Influence People,* Dale Carnegie talks about the importance of being the kind of person who helps people meet their needs and achieve their goals. Most people are not used to encountering folks who are willing to help them get where they are trying to go. By actively seeking opportunities to become such a person, you will not only win friends, but you will also be able to influence people to treat you with the respect and cooperation you seek.

Assert more respectful and efficient ways to meet the need or intention.

Once you have convinced a person that you are on her side and are willing to help her meet her needs or fulfill her positive intentions, the fun begins. It is at this stage of the game that you begin to work toward solutions by suggesting more respectful and efficient ways for the person to get what he or she wants.

In the example of Jerry and Linda, Linda was distancing herself from Jerry in order to protect herself from what she experienced as his negativity. Jerry did not experience himself as being particularly negative, but he was willing to accept that perhaps he occasionally and unintentionally came across that way. Even more important, he agreed with Linda that she shouldn't have to put up with undue negativity in her life. So in our sessions he asked if, rather than distancing herself from him, she would be willing to point out—in the moment—when he was being negative. This way, he could better understand what she was talking about and either correct her perception or change his behavior. By making this suggestion, Jerry offered a more respectful and efficient way for Linda to meet her intention, and although she wasn't sure at first whether or not she should believe him, she agreed that if he could pull it off, she would prefer that option to having to distance herself from him. In a matter of weeks, Linda and Jerry felt closer to one another than they had in years, and what seemed to accomplish this, more than anything else, was Jerry's suggestion of a more efficient and respectful way for Linda to get what she needed from him.

Likewise, when Gina was able to understand that Merrill's behavior (keeping the door closed, being aloof) was her way of making herself feel more comfortable in what was, to her, an awkward and even painful social situation, Gina was able to offer her friendship as way to help Merrill feel more comfortable. When Gina expressed her willingness to run interference for Merrill at the office, Merrill was freed up to be a little more relaxed around her coworkers, doing things like keeping the door open, bringing in doughnuts occasionally, and even, over time, making small talk.

Creating respectful change in others is much easier than most people think it is. All you have to do is take the time to learn what another person's intentions really are and then suggest more efficient and respectful ways to fulfill those intentions. Think about it; if you were beating your head into a door to open it, wouldn't you be grateful if someone were to come along with a key? Instead of being paranoid and defensive about the ham-fisted ways people (including yourself) go about trying to meet their needs, you can approach such situations with compassion and a gentle sense of humor. You can suggest ways to help them meet their needs in a manner that is easier on themselves and on the people around them, and they will be grateful to you for your interest and generosity. Similarly, they will use those ways in the future, making your life a lot easier in the process.

Create a plan to help each other use these new, more respectful strategies.

Once you and the other person have arrived at more respectful and efficient ways to meet his needs, you will need to come up with a plan for keeping each other on track. Too often in problem solving, we think that telling a person once should be enough for the rest of his life. Then, the first time he has a bad day and forgets to do what we discussed, we write him off as the idiot we always secretly suspected him to be.

When I am nearing the end of counseling with my clients, I always spend at least a session or two talking about how they will manage to keep the changes they have made for the rest of their life. Usually, this doesn't involve too much, for once a new behavior becomes a habit (this usually takes about two weeks to a month), the behavior becomes self-sustaining. But until that time, it is easy to forget all the new things they have learned, and when they do, they revert—quite unintentionally and unconsciously—to the old, inefficient, and stupid ways of doing things.

Now, I could tell my clients how they should behave differently. I could talk about it until they agree to do what I am suggesting, and then I could pronounce them cured. Then, a week later, when they have slipped up a couple of times, I could insult them and tell them that they clearly don't care about me or anything I have to say and that unless they shape up, I am not going to have anything else to do with them. I could do this, but doing so would make me not only a lousy counselor, but a fairly despicable human being too.

And yet, we all (yours truly included) do exactly this in our personal relationships. When we want someone to change, we want it yesterday. Oh, we'll be big about it if we have to be and hang in there until the person we are struggling with seems to get it. But once we arrive at a solution, God forbid that person would ever have a bad day and forget to do what they agreed to do, instead reverting to his or her old habit. Then we would feel *betrayed! Betrayed,* I tell you!

The only thing being betrayed is our own irrationality. No, the ultimate change should not take years to achieve, and yes, we should be able to see the other person making a sincere effort to change, but assuming that these two things are true, we need to find respectful ways to assist him in the struggle to change. This is another example of what it means to practice Christian love, to work for the good of another. While you are not obliged to stand by someone who isn't even trying, you are obliged to go to the mat for someone who is sincerely struggling. This, I believe, is what the Lord really means when he says that we are to forgive another person "seventy times seven" times.

To this end, once a person agrees to change, we need to take a minute and ask ourselves, "What can we do to keep each other honest?" What can you do to help the other person remember what you agreed on, and what can he do to let you know if you are being unreasonably impatient with him and his struggle?

Toward the end of their counseling, Diana and Bud had a bad spell. They had entered therapy because Diana had felt that Bud was taking her for granted, and vice versa. During counseling, things had gotten significantly better, but in the two weeks between their last sessions, the relationship had experienced a downslide. Diana, a CPA, had been working late every evening doing end-of-the-quarter work for her clients. Once, she had to cancel a scheduled date with Bud, and other nights when she got home she was often too tired to do anything except go to bed. Rather than talking directly to Diana about his feelings and using the strategies for keeping each other on track with what they had discussed in counseling, Bud gave into his fear of being taken advantage of. One night, he accused her of wasting their time and money on counseling that, to his mind at that time, "didn't do any damn good since you are going to do what you want anyway once we stop!" Diana was more than a little wounded by this exchange, but fortunately they were able to make it to the next session, albeit in a somewhat rattled state.

In that meeting, I was able to ascertain that each really was committed to following the plan we had developed, but that the busyness Diana had encountered over the past few weeks had thrown her for a loop. Once more, both she and Bud expressed their desire to do whatever it took to get things back on track. I reminded them that, rather than get offended if one or the other of them was forgetting to do the things we had discussed in counseling, they should stick with their promise to each other to simply say, "I really miss you and I'm afraid we're going to start taking each other for granted again. How can we get back on track?"

They both agreed that this would be an effective alternative to the "pout-fest," as Bud had taken to calling it. Within a few weeks, they had restored order to the marriage, even though each had to remind the other at times to follow up on his or her intentions to make the marriage better.

When you and the other person finally do work out a more respectful way to relate to each other, be realistic about the need to remind each other, respectfully and openly, to follow the plan and be patient with the change process.

Evaluate the results and make adjustments as needed.

Finally, after a couple of weeks of consistently living out the solution you and the other person have arrived at, you will want to evaluate whether or not the new solution is working. If it is, congratulations! Your work is done. But if it is not working, or if you continue to feel uncomfortable with the other person, consider this.

The most likely explanation for this process not working is that it failed to address the true intention of the original problem behavior. Similarly, your solution may have addressed only one of many intentions the person was trying to meet by acting offensively (this is often the case with compulsive behaviors such as habits and addictions). Use one of the two tools mentioned in the beginning of the chapter to reassess the intention(s) behind the continuing problem behavior and repeat the five steps of the P-E-A-C-E process. ("You know, I thought we worked through this, but maybe we missed something. What [else] do you gain by continuing to use that old way of acting/speaking with me?")

Alternatively, if you have used this method several times and the person continues to act in an offensive way regardless of what he promises, perhaps the problem is bigger than you can handle on your own. In such instances, you may be required to enlist the help of a professional counselor, or when this is not possible, you may simply have to set some limits and decrease the importance of this relationship in your life (see the next chapter).

Before you set limits or distance yourself from someone, however, it is important for you to remember that, according to Christian Scriptures at least, you have an obligation to make every reasonable effort to resolve the dispute before terminating the relationship. This is clear in the New Testament (Matthew 18:15–17), which goes so far as to outline how to deal with a difficult relationship. According to Scripture, if we fail to resolve the problem on our own, our next step is to seek some kind of friendly mediation (Scripture refers to the elders of the church, but practically speaking, this could just as easily be your pastor or a close and mutually respected friend). If this fails, then the next step is to seek professional guidance. Scripture refers to the courts, but the courts of Jesus' time were not the adversarial courts we have in America today. They were more like professional mediation or counseling. Only after we have exhausted all reasonable means available to us and if the other person is still resistant to working with us are we permitted to end the relationship. This is a wise process, because on the one hand, it prevents us from writing people off too quickly. On the other hand, it makes certain that we are not obliging ourselves to be the perpetual victims of people who will not change under any circumstances.

Before we bring this chapter to a close, I invite you to review the five steps of the P-E-A-C-E process by completing the following exercise.

REVIEWING THE P-E-A-C-E PROCESS: AN EXERCISE

Choose a problem situation. Write it down.

Step One: Practice working with, not against, each other. Remember, the person is never the problem; the problem is the problem. Work with your teammate to resolve the problem. Answer this question: What will you need to do to see this person as a teammate rather than an enemy?

Step Two: Express your desire to help the other person meet his or her need or intention. Reassure the person that you want to do whatever it takes to help meet this need or fulfill this intention as long as he or she is willing to work with you to find more respectful and efficient ways to do it.

By using one of the techniques presented earlier in this chapter (either "the direct approach" or "follow the money"), assess the positive intention behind the offensive behavior. Write it down.

What steps will you take to reassure the other person that you value the intention he or she is trying to fulfill or the need he or she is trying to meet? Write down your ideas.

Step Three: Assert more respectful and efficient ways to meet the need or intention. Brainstorm and list some respectful and efficient ways to meet the intention or need. Include the other person's ideas as well as your own.

Step Four: Create a plan to help each other use these new, more respectful strategies. Once you have agreed on a solution, determine how you will keep each other on track. How can you respectfully (without resentment or huffiness) remind the other person to stick to the plan? How can the other person respectfully let you know if you are being too impatient with his or her struggle? Write down your ideas.

Step Five: Evaluate the results and make adjustments as needed. It can take two weeks to a month for a new behavior to become a habit. After you and your partner have attempted to carry out your plan for that period of time, evaluate your success. Which of the following is true?

- Everyone is satisfied with the change. Your work is done.
- One or both of you is dissatisfied with the results. Reassess the intention or need behind the behavior and go through the P-E-A-C-E process again.
- Either you have attempted but failed to engage the other person in the P-E-A-C-E process or, despite sincere, mutual effort, the process is not working. Consider seeking professional help. Contact the Pastoral Solutions Institute at (740) 266-6461 for assistance or a referral.*

Keep the Change

When I first present these methods, many people find them interesting, but they wonder if change can really be that easy. Isn't change supposed to be hard? No pain, no gain, right?

Well, not really. Change can be the easiest thing in the world, if it is respectful and efficient enough. And just because a problem has existed for

* If counseling is not an option, use the limit-setting strategies in chapter 6 .

a long time doesn't mean that it has to take a long time to change it. Let me give you an example.

Imagine that you have been driving to work the same way for twenty years and that every day it takes you an hour—door to door. Now imagine that I take out a map and show you a new road that will get you there in half the time. Wouldn't you take that new way immediately? Moreover, the new way would be so much more efficient, so much more respectful of your time that you probably wouldn't ever think about going the old way again. Oh, one day you might go down the old road because you aren't thinking, but that probably won't happen more than once or twice before you correct your behavior permanently. The new way is just too good to pass up.

The same philosophy applies to the kind of change we are looking to create with the methods outlined in this chapter. It is possible to create alternative methods of behaving that are so much more respectful, efficient, and rewarding that only a fool would persist in the old, inefficient, offensive patterns. And if the person really is that big of a fool, you will either need professional help to deal with her or, failing that, you will need to set limits and/or distance yourself from her. That said, most people will change given the chance, especially if you show them a truly more effective way to get what they want out of life. People long to be liked, but their need to have their needs met is even stronger. If you can show a person how to meet her needs *and* become a more likeable person in the process, most likely she will jump at the chance. Wouldn't you?

Not every problem will be resolved by using the techniques presented in this chapter, but many can be, as long as you keep your own head about you and remember that behind every behavior—especially the offensive, obnoxious, sinful, and destructive behaviors—is a God-given need or positive intention attempting to be expressed. If you can discover that need or intention, you will be on the road to creating lasting, respectful change.

The Secrets of Winning Every Time: How to Keep Relationships on Course

Anybody can become angry—that is easy; but to be angry with the right person, and to the right degree, and at the right time, and for the right purpose, and in the right way—that ...is not easy.

~ ARISTOTLE
From Nicomachean Ethics

Now that we've looked at the most powerful techniques to effect change—looking for the positive intention behind offensive behavior and using the P-E-A-C-E process—I want to introduce you to the five strategies that will help you work with almost anyone to solve almost any problem.

These strategies go hand in hand with the P-E-A-C-E process, because you cannot effectively use the P-E-A-C-E process without them. Moreover, you cannot effectively use the techniques I will present in this chapter without first understanding how to discover the positive intention behind offensive behavior.

Counselors and others often seek to prescribe rules for effective problem solving, suggesting things like "Don't go to bed angry" or "Take breaks when arguments are getting out of hand." But it has been my experience that unless you really understand that the person you are arguing with is not out to get you—which is only possible if you are able to assume that the other person has a positive motivation for acting as he does—then all the rules fly out the window.

Assuming, however, that you are now a master of liberality and a skilled practitioner of the art of looking for a positive intention behind the offensive actions of others, I would like to introduce five strategies that will help you work with almost anyone to solve almost any problem.

Strategies for Problem Solving

- Watch your emotional temperature.
- Take respectful breaks.
- Encourage teamwork.
- Never negotiate the "what." Always negotiate the "how" and "when."
- Maintain your emotional bank account.

Let's take a look at each of these strategies.

Watch your emotional temperature.

Think of a scale from 1 to 10. One represents you on heavy tranquilizers, 4 represents you in a calm but alert state, and 10 represents you climbing a clock tower with an AK-47 strapped to your back. On this type of scale, no productive discussion between two people can happen if one or both of you register at over 6.5.

At that point, your fight-or-flight response kicks in, your heart rate increases rapidly from 80 beats per minute to upwards of 120 beats per minute, and your discussion begins to devolve into something resembling *War of the Worlds*, only without all the aliens.

All right, that was the humorous overview. Let me try to make this a bit more practical. Imagine that you and I are having a disagreement. At 5 on our emotional-temperature scale, we are getting along well, being more or less civil to one another, and things are being accomplished. At around 6, you might notice yourself engaging in some stress behavior, such as jiggling your knee, straightening things in front of you, and fighting the urge to pace, but things are still basically under control. At 6.5, you start to suspect that I might indeed be an idiot of one sort or another, but you are still willing to give me the benefit of the doubt—and you are still being outwardly civil. When we reach 7, you have decided that I am definitely an idiot and you may begin rolling your eyes and huffing and puffing at me and thinking of a few choice names you would like to call me. Granted, you aren't calling me those names (well, one or two might slip out), but it is obvious to everyone around that you have had it with me. If we allow the argument to go to 8, we are officially "having words," most of which are unkind—or at least unproductive. Those unkind names you were thinking of calling me are now verbally replacing the one my mother gave me. At 9, you are either beginning to retreat into your cave to escape the stress or you are thinking about punching a hole in the wall. And at 10, you have either buried yourself so deeply in that cave that I can't get to you or you have made a hole in the wall.

You get the point.

The trick to successful negotiation is catching yourself at 6.5 or lower. Most people are at the point of screaming or running away (about an 8 on the scale) before they realize that the "discussion" is getting out of hand. This is entirely too late. Really, the discussion is already beginning to get too hot at one of two points: when you catch yourself engaging in your stress behavior (one of my stress behaviors is absentmindedly making whatever happens to be in front of me into a neat pile) *or* when you begin attributing a negative intention to the other person's behavior. The second you begin to think, *This person is not only as dumb as a brick, but he's out to get me too!* (admit it, we all think this way from time to time), you know that you are allowing your emotional temperature to rise too high. If you get to that point, you will have to quickly engage in some cool-down strategies (see following pages) if you want to continue a productive discussion. This is especially true if you are using the P-E-A-C-E process, which will only work if both parties believe that each is sincerely looking out for the other's good. This is impossible to feel if you are getting those "dumb as a brick" vibes from your sparring partner.

Before going any further, take a moment to identify your stress behavior or the kinds of thoughts that go through your head as you begin approaching a 6.5 on the emotional-temperature scale. If you are having difficulty identifying either the stress habit you have or "the look" you get when you are stressed, ask someone close to you who has seen you when you are upset to tell you what kind of behavioral signals you send out to let people know when you are reaching critical mass. Write them down.

Let these behaviors serve as your signal that you are beginning to get too stressed to have a productive discussion and that you need to find a way to reduce your emotional fever before you burn up.

One of the best frontline tools for maintaining a productive emotional temperature is to ask plenty of clarifying questions. You may remember some of these from an earlier chapter. A clarifying question looks like this: "When you told me I was thoughtless (state the offensive behavior), I really felt like you were trying to hurt my feelings (offer your interpretation). Is that what you were trying to do (give the benefit of the doubt)?"

When you ask a clarifying question, you accomplish three things. First, you reinforce the need for both you and the other person to look for the positive intention behind the offense. Second, you use a respectful method for letting the other person know when he or she is crossing the line. And third, you give the other person the opportunity to correct the faux pas in order to move the discussion along.

Sometimes people will tell me that they, or someone close to them, have a hair-trigger temper that seems to go from 1 to 10 in no time. Often, this is because such people never begin to talk about a problem until they are already at a 7 or higher and they can't take the pressure anymore. Because they are already stressed when the discussion begins, it doesn't take much for it to get completely out of control. Another reason that their temper accelerates too quickly is that they have had life experiences that have made them overly sensitive to criticism or distrustful of others. When this is the case, counseling may be needed.

Besides asking clarifying questions, the two techniques that follow are also good ways to reduce emotional fevers.

Take respectful breaks.

The second strategy for effective problem solving is remembering to take respectful breaks. Many people think that taking breaks in an argument means waiting until you are screaming at each other and then either stopping the discussion cold or just walking away (often while the other person chases you from room to room trying to have his or her say). Either way, most of these "breaks" last for hours if not days and include a great deal of bitter feelings. It should be obvious to you that neither of these options is what I would call a respectful break.

A respectful break is what should occur at around a 6.5 on the temperature scale. At that level, a break might last for only a few minutes, but it will still be a very effective way to decrease the tension. When you catch yourself engaging in the stress behavior you just identified, do something to break up the conversation for a moment. Excuse yourself and go to the bathroom, get up to get a drink (and offer your partner one as well), ask for a hug, or offer the other person a piece of pie—anything to interrupt the flow momentarily. Even these simple breaks can be enough to keep a problem-solving discussion on track.

Of course, if you are becoming really stressed by a discussion and do need to take a longer break, the best way to express this is to say something like "Obviously, we need to talk about this some more, but would you mind if we took a break right now and picked it up (offer specific time)? I'm just starting to feel overwhelmed and I don't think I can keep going."

You should feel free to use your own words, but make sure that whatever you say, you let the other person know that you really do want to keep dealing with this issue and you aren't just trying to weasel out of the discussion. Offer a specific time to pick up the discussion. This could be as formal as putting a time on the calendar or as informal as saying, "Let's talk about this again tomorrow afternoon." But make sure that you offer a specific time. This reinforces the idea that you really are willing to take up the topic. It also decreases the chances that the other person will follow you around from room to room or hunt you down to remind you that you still have to discuss his or her concerns.

You need to think of your personal arguments as more like business meetings, where people get together to solve a problem. At no time during a business discussion would you find it appropriate to suggest that a coworker was "just like his crazy bitch of a mother!" Even so, the fact that this behavior isn't appropriate doesn't seem to stop us from threatening, name-calling, whining, begging, or otherwise losing it in our personal problem-solving sessions. When you get in the habit of taking respectful breaks, your personal discussions will flow more like business meetings, where you accomplish a certain amount of work, get tired or stressed, take a break, come back and work some more, take another break, and so on until the job is done. There is an old joke,

"How do you eat an elephant?"

"One piece at a time."

This is also true of our personal struggles with others. When we deal with hot topics on a personal level, we have a tendency to want to solve everything right now. This rarely happens. Taking breaks allows two people to collect their thoughts, to focus on one issue at a time, and to remember that they are supposed to be working as a team.

Encourage teamwork.

When you are struggling to solve a problem, the one thing that is always more important than solving the problem is taking care of your teammate. If the person with whom you are trying to resolve an issue does not feel like a teammate, then chances are you are doing it wrong.

Granted, some people simply will not work with you no matter what, but this is not most people. The better you become at using the techniques in this book, the more you will encounter people who are willing to cooperate with you to meet needs and solve problems.

When you are struggling to solve a problem with someone, do your best to let him or her know that getting through the tension *with your relationship intact* is of primary importance to you. The simplest way to do this is to use words that encourage you toward a solution instead of those that encourage you to take up arms against each other. Compare the two columns below and you'll see what I mean.

Encouragin' Words	(Them's) Fightin' Words
What did you mean when you said that?	I can't believe you did/said that!
I don't understand.	What's wrong with you?
Thanks for hanging in there with me even when things get tense.	You're getting on my nerves.
What do we need to do to get through this?	You are so stubborn!
I need to take a quick break. I'll be right back.	Just leave me alone!
Let's just try to stay focused. I know we can get through this.	I'm sick of having the same argument over and over again.
We need to keep talking about this, but could we pick it up (insert time here)?	I'm not going to discuss this anymore.
Look, our relationship means a lot to me. Let's try to make it through this in one piece.	I don't care what you think!
We've made it through plenty of tough times; I'm sure we'll find a way through this too.	All we ever do is fight.

The difference is clear, isn't it? Recently, I was talking with a man, Gil, who was upset about the way his wife disciplined their children. He told me that she lost her cool fairly quickly, especially with one child in particular who was most capable of pushing her buttons. Gil's usual method of responding to the problem was to jump into the fray and say, "Don't talk to our kids that way! What's wrong with you?" He would then take over the interaction with the children and cut his wife out. "After all," he explained, "I can't just stand there and let my wife destroy our child's self-esteem." His major issue, however, was his frustration at his wife for not appreciating his "help" in these situations. "She just yells at me and tells me I'm undermining her authority. And I'll be damned if I don't keep undermining it if she is going to act that way!"

Fortunately, I was seeing his wife in counseling too, so I knew that she wasn't doing anything abusive, although I also knew that she often felt at the end of her tether. I told Gil that I appreciated his need to nurture his kid's self-esteem (I validated the positive intention behind his clumsy effort), but I could think of another way to do it. I told him that the next time he saw his wife losing it, he should go up to her, give her a gentle hug, and say in a compassionate tone of voice, "You really seem stressed out. What can I do to help?" This way, he could send the message that she wasn't exactly handling things well at the moment and that he was not there to criticize but to help. Gil seemed a little suspicious of my suggestion, but he said he would try it "as an experiment."

The next week, Gil told me that the new approach worked great. In fact, the first time he did it, his wife started to cry. Instead of yelling at him, she thanked him for trying so hard and asked him to take over for a minute while she took a short break. The funny thing is that the rest of the week things were a lot calmer in general. When Gil asked about the change in her demeanor, she said that just knowing he was on her side helped her handle the kids better. By intervening the way I asked him to instead of merely jumping in and taking over, he found a way to take what was a tense and alienating situation and transform it into an opportunity to build intimacy. The lesson for all of us in this story is to never underestimate the power of words. How you say things really does matter. So when you need to make a criticism or call attention to a problem, avoid coming across like the expert. Instead, work hard to come across as a friend who needs or wants to give help.

Never negotiate the "what." Always negotiate the "how" and "when." This is a biggie.

Most adult arguments occur when one person tells another person that what he or she wants is silly or unrealistic.

"What do you mean you want me to be more affectionate?"

"We don't have the money for that!"

"Nobody in their right mind would ever want that! What's wrong with you?"

Respectful problem solvers try to avoid such approaches because these approaches tend to breed resentment and anger. That is, respectful problem solvers never argue about what you want. They simply negotiate the how and the when of meeting your need. Let me give you an example.

Imagine that your teenager comes to you and asks for a $120 pair of sneakers. Your first inclination would probably be to say the same thing I would say: "What?! Are you out of your trees?" But this is an example of negotiating the what. You are trying to talk your child out of something he wants—and in the process missing out on an opportunity to teach responsibility. Don't negotiate the what (whether he should or should not want such a thing). Instead, negotiate the conditions or the time frame under which he might be able to acquire such a thing. You could say, "I have forty dollars for a pair of gym shoes. If you want the more expensive ones, you will have to spend your own money to make up the difference." If your adolescent doesn't have his own money, maybe it's time he got a job. You could suggest that one way he could make the extra money needed for the pair of shoes would be to get a job. Another alternative—if you were so inclined—would be to say that even though you don't have the money now, perhaps, if he really wants them, they could be his birthday present instead of something else he asked for. These are both examples of negotiating the how and the when. Instead of merely saying no, you give a qualified yes. You, in effect, say to the other person, "I cannot give you what you are asking for on your terms because of certain concerns that I have, but here are some terms by which you might be able to get the thing you're after." Then you let the other person decide how important it is to him or her.

This strategy is useful in the workplace as well. For example, if an employee goes to her boss and asks for a raise, initially the boss might be inclined to say, "I'm sorry, but there just isn't any money in the budget for that right now." But the effective manager will more likely say, "I would be willing to give you a raise, but here are my concerns...." The manager and the employee could then work together to develop a plan for addressing those concerns. Perhaps the employee needs to have a higher sales ratio; perhaps her raise would be better justified if her productivity were higher or if she took on additional responsibilities at the office. In any case, even if the employee ends up deciding that too much work is involved in getting the raise, she will not come to resent her manager, because her manager was willing to work with her to help her get what she wanted. The manager did not negotiate the what (the raise). She simply negotiated the how and the when (the concerns that needed to be addressed in order for the raise to be granted.)

If it is often advisable—although it is sometimes impossible or impractical—to use this strategy with friends, employees, or even children, it is absolutely essential to use it in your marriage. Under no circumstances should you ever put yourself in the position of giving or denying your spouse permission to go after something he or she wants, be it a thing, a personal goal, a certain amount of time or attention, or an emotional investment on your part. Negotiating the what (instead of the how and when) in marriage changes you from a partner into a parent, and it reduces your spouse from an adult to a child. Inevitably, this dynamic creates the kind of resentment that, if allowed to go unchecked, causes divorce. Let's look at another example, this time a silly one.

Imagine that you and I are married and you tell me that you want to move to Australia and start an ostrich ranch. (Believe it or not, this actually happened to someone I know.) Now, granted, any person's normal reaction to this would be "What! Are you nuts?" Even so, your reaction to my saying such a thing—because your heart and future happiness are really set on herding ostriches in the Australian outback—would be resentment and anger: "How dare you stand between me and my dreams!"

Now, I care very deeply for you (you know I do!) and I would never want you to feel that I was standing between you and your dreams. So, for the sake of argument, let's apply the "never negotiate the what" rule to this situation. Instead of telling you that not only is there no way in the world I am going to be your partner in this ridiculous venture, but I also think that you are the biggest idiot that ever walked on two legs, I am going to assume that you are an adult with God-given intelligence and I am going to hear you out. Then I am going to say something like this: "Well, I would be lying if I didn't say I have some serious questions, but I'll tell you this: if you can come up with a workable plan that actually addresses my concerns, I would be willing to support you." Then I would go on to ask you a series of questions, such as "How would we make a living?" "How could I move my counseling practice to Australia?" "How would you reckon with my allergies to ostrich-egg omelets?" (I told you this was a silly example.) I am going to lay out all of my concerns, all of the needs I feel would go unmet if I supported this crazy idea of yours. Then the ball is in your court. If you can show me a convincing plan for pursuing your dream while meeting all of my needs and concerns, then I will be all for it. On the other hand, you might just as well decide that it costs too much to fulfill the dream you have of taking on the outback with the ostriches. Either way, it's your decision, and whether you go ahead with the plan or not, you will come to thank me for helping you bring more clarity to the process.

Now, your spouse may never ask you to help her start an ostrich farm. But she may want to do something that you think is almost as harebrained. She may ask you to support her in her dream of owning her own business. Or she may ask you for more time and attention. Or she may ask you to stay home and not go out with your other friends tonight. Or she may tell you that she wants another child. In most cases, too many spouses try to negotiate the what. They say, "Are you nuts? What's wrong with you? Why would you ever want that?" This is not to say that these same spouses may not have some very legitimate concerns, but what I am talking about is different from denying your spouse something because of those concerns. Under such conditions, it is so much better to simply negotiate the how and the when, to say, "I would be willing to support you in that, but here are my concerns...If and when we can come up with a workable plan for meeting those concerns, then you should absolutely do/get what you're telling me about."

Please understand that negotiating the how and the when is not the same as engaging in quid pro quo negotiations. Sometimes when I describe this process, people think I mean that they should adopt an "If you scratch my back, I'll scratch yours" attitude. I don't mean that at all. While it may not be universally true, it has been my experience that people who engage in these tit-for-tat discussions are really lacking in Christian generosity. In dealing with them you get the impression that they are always asking, "What's in it for me?"

This was the case with one couple I knew. Erin wanted a new house. Charles wanted a new baby. They argued about both things for months. Finally, Erin said, "Look, if you get me the house, we can try to have another baby." Charles agreed, and one year later they had both.

While both seemed happy enough with their "arrangement," frankly, the whole thing struck me as remarkably distasteful. So-called negotiations like this just stink of mutual manipulation and are, in my opinion, demeaning to both parties even when they don't involve such huge topics. In the case of Erin and Charles, it would have been so much better to treat the baby and the house as two separate issues and to negotiate the how and the when for each. For example, Erin could have said, "I would be willing to have another baby, but here are my concerns...If we can find a way to address these concerns, then we can get to work right away—but not before." And Charles could have said, "I would be willing to look into a new house, but here are my concerns...If we could come up with a plan to overcome them, then I'll call the real estate agent myself!" Either of these statements is much more respectful and honest than the "trading" Erin and Charles were participating in.

Negotiating the how and the when does not mean saying, "If you give me something I want, I'll give you something you want." It means that I am willing to do anything I can to support you in the pursuit of your dreams, goals, and values as long as you are respectful of mine as well. Following this principle of negotiating not the what but the when and how allows two people to help each other fulfill all of their needs and their most important wants while respecting and nurturing the relationship at the same time.

Maintain your emotional bank account.

In recent years, it has become popular to speak of relationships as "emotional bank accounts." If you have a real bank account, you make certain that you don't spend more than you deposit. If you do overspend, the bank might extend you some credit, but it won't give you much, and your overspending will cost you in the end. In the same way, with relationships, you want to make certain that you deposit more emotional currency than you spend, because if you don't, you will run out of credit (or in the case of relationships, credibility) very fast. So every time you give a compliment, do something kind, or offer help or support, you make a deposit into the emotional bank account you keep with another person. Likewise, when you ask for a favor, criticize, raise a complaint, argue, or have a disagreement, you make withdrawals from the emotional bank account. There is nothing wrong with making withdrawals (offering constructive criticisms, asking other people to change or to put themselves out in some way for your sake)—that is what the money is there for, after all. But it is important to make sure that you are much more liberal with words of encouragement, acts of service, and compliments than you are with criticisms, complaints, or requests for help. If you aren't, your problem-solving methods will break down quickly, and pretty soon you and the other person will be at each other's throats. You will begin thinking of him as an insensitive jerk who doesn't care about anyone other than himself, and he will begin thinking of you as someone who only nags, whines, or complains. Obviously, this does not establish a good environment for change.

In the mid-1990s, Dr. John Gottman did a study on marriage. He was able to predict with 95 percent accuracy which couples would be together in five years and which couples would be divorced or divorcing in five years. His study revealed that those couples who were still together had maintained a 5:1 ratio of positivity to negativity in their relationship. That is, even though some of these couples argued—a lot—the arguments were absorbed more easily because they were five times more passionate, complimentary, supportive, affectionate, and helpful to each other than they were negative toward each other. Conversely, those couples who did not maintain this ratio in their marriage became progressively more hostile, defensive, and resentful of each other. Why? Because if I know that my wife is looking out for my best interest eight times out of ten, then I am willing to give her the benefit of the doubt the other two times when I am not so sure where she is coming from. On the other hand, if that positivity-to-negativity ratio shifts to 3:1 or to 1:1, or even to 1:3, then all of a sudden I'm not sure my wife really cares about me (and vice versa), and an attitude of "everyone for him- or herself" permeates the relationship.

Interestingly, I have observed that this 5:1 positivity-to-negativity ratio has ramifications beyond marriage. Because people are more or less the same regardless of the relationship they find themselves in, this ratio has almost universal applications. I have noticed that if parents and children, employers and employees (as well as coworkers), friends and companions maintain a similar ratio, then these individuals report being satisfied in these relationships. By contrast, when the 5:1 ratio (or, as Dr. Gottman called it, "the magic number") is violated in these relationships, hostility, defensiveness, and resentment build almost exponentially.

Think for a moment about the problem relationships in your life. Ask yourself these questions: Am I maintaining the magic number in these relationships? Am I five times more complimentary, helpful, generous, supportive, and kind than I am demanding, complaining, critical, and cross? Chances are, the answer is no. I would suggest that this is the reason for the breakdown in communication.

I know, I know. The other person isn't being nice to you either. I sympathize, but that is entirely beside the point. If you have decided that for some reason this relationship is important to you, then you have no other choice but to continue to nurture the relationship even while you wait for change. Later on you will have an opportunity to assess whether or not it would be better to simply limit or end the relationship. But for now we are still trying to change things for the better, and you simply cannot do this unless you are working to maintain the rapport between yourself and the person you must partner with in order to solve problems.

Even if he or she is not exactly being nice to you, your first tack should be to try to build rapport. (Note that building rapport is not the issue if you are being physically or verbally abused.) Stop complaining for a while and decide to work on rebuilding (or building) your friendship with the other person. In her book *Raising Catholic Children,* Mary Ann Kuharski, a mother of thirteen, tells the story of a family who was having a terrible time with a teenaged son who was all but completely estranged from the family. They had tried everything, even counseling, with no success. Finally one therapist suggested that the first thing the parents needed to do was stop all verbal communication and increase the amount of physical affection they gave their son. As the mother told Ms. Kuharski,

> *After two weeks of virtually forcing a daily hug I saw no real warmth or change. Late one evening of the second week, however, he came up behind me while I was reading a newspaper...I asked him what he was looking for. He shrugged and sheepishly said, "Aren't you*

forgetting something?" (referring to the good-night hug I'd usually given him).

It worked! When talking, screaming, crying, and nagging had done nothing but aggravate a hostile situation, a daily hug had melted hearts and broken down barriers.

As you can see, affection and rapport are everything. If you are having problems with your spouse, begin doing the loving, generous, and kind things you should have been doing all along, not necessarily because you feel like it or because you think he or she deserves it, but because it is beneath your Christian dignity to act in any other way. If you are having problems with your children, ask yourself if you might be better off if you took a break from yelling at them so much and actually spent a bit more time hugging them or playing the games they want to play. If you are having difficulties at work, before you go into the office demanding change, till the soil a bit by working to become the person who brings doughnuts in the morning, offers to stop and pick up things for coworkers on the way back from lunch, or at least notices when someone has changed his or her hair, is wearing an especially nice shirt, or has done a particularly good job.

This might seem like so much silliness to you, especially if you are frustrated. You don't want to have to stop complaining; you want results. I sympathize. I once described to a client the need to work on the 5:1 ratio in her marriage, and she interrupted me, saying, "So, basically, I'm paying you to tell me that I should try to be nice to my husband." She, like many of us, didn't want to hear that the reason things were not changing in her marriage was that she lacked the credibility required to effect a change. Like it or not, you cannot create change without first having a solid relationship. Of course, "being nice" is not the be-all and end-all. You still must assert yourself when your own needs are being neglected or your dignity is being trampled upon. But you will not be able to do this effectively unless and until you have earned credibility, and you do this by going out of your way to show the people around you that you care. Truth be told, most people do not change for any other reason than that they are afraid of losing a relationship they value.

Even God recognizes this fact and lives by this rule—at least as far as his relationship with us goes. After all, the whole point of Jesus dwelling on earth as God in the flesh, not to mention Jesus' suffering, death, and resurrection, is to establish a relationship the like of which has been unheard of throughout history. Once this relationship was established, God then had the "credibility" to tell us, "Take up your cross and follow me." Jesus became a human being and so knew how human beings operate. He also knew that asking us to make a big change required a big investment on his part, which is why, even today, we sing, "Oh, how I love Jesus *because he first loved me.*" Our obedience to God—our willingness to enact the changes God asks of us—is our response to God's having loved us first. In the same way, our ability to command the obedience of others—be they our friends, spouse, children, or coworkers—is directly proportional to our ability to build up our side of the 5:1 ratio even if we don't feel like it, even when the other person does not deserve such generosity. We do this because our God first did it for us and then commanded us to go out and do the same for the world.

Before we close out this chapter, complete the following exercise to see if you are missing out on opportunities to build rapport with the difficult people in your life, rapport that serves as the foundation and catalyst for future change.

OH, HOW I CAN CHANGE THEM, BECAUSE I FIRST CHANGED ME: AN EXERCISE

Identify someone with whom you struggle. Ideally, this should be a person who you believe is basically decent and probably has a good heart, but who, for some reason, you can't seem to work with. Write down this person's name.

What kinds of changes would you like to see in this person? What kinds of changes would make the relationship go easier for you? (That is, what changes do you want him or her to make?) Write these down.

The list you just made represents the kinds of changes you can ask for after you have built rapport with the other person. Now, take a minute to ask yourself the following two questions and to write down the answers.

- What kinds of things do I do for those people I get along with, but don't do for this person?
- What has this person asked me to do for him or her in the past, but I have not done because I didn't feel that he or she deserved the effort?

The items you've just listed are the things you must bring yourself to do in order to build the rapport you must have before you can get the changes you want. Now, rate your relationship with this person. Is it on life support, or strained but still basically cordial?

If your relationship is on life support, you will need to spend the next two to three weeks doing those things you just listed—without asking anything in return—before you can even bring up the changes you want from the other person. Even if your relationship is merely strained but still cordial, you will still need to do the things you listed for at least two weeks before you can bring up the changes you want from him or her.

It is especially important that you continue doing these things even after you ask your partner to make certain changes. Otherwise your efforts will be dismissed, because it will seem that you were only trying to butter up the other person to get something out of him.

How Does Your Garden Grow?

Think of creating change as planting a garden. In a garden, first you must till the soil. Then you can plant the seed. But even after you plant the seed, you need to continue tending the garden. In the same way, you must till the soil of the relationship (build rapport) before you can plant the seeds of change (ask for what you want from the other person). But even after you plant the seed, you must tend the garden by continuing to do the things necessary to maintain rapport. If you don't keep tending the plants—maintaining rapport—the seeds of change will die before they sprout, or too soon afterward.

Many people prefer to simply throw their seeds on untilled soil and then scream at, nag, demean, or pick on their partner to make the seeds grow. This never works. Other people will go through the trouble of tilling the soil and planting the seeds, but then think the seeds should grow all by themselves. These people come to resent their garden because sprouts keep shooting up and then dying (the other person changes for a week and then goes back to the same old ways). They blame the seed or the garden, forgetting that, in fact, it is their own neglect (failing to continue to do what they must do to maintain rapport) that causes the seeds to starve to death. Only the people who are willing to put all the work into the garden—tilling, planting, and tending—can enjoy the harvest of change.

This takes work and maturity. If you are not willing to work for the changes in your life or if you lack the maturity to follow through on your efforts, you can hardly resent somebody else for not changing. It will be necessary for you to work on yourself first.

There will always be certain people who are completely resistant to love. While this is not as common as we might think, it is certainly more common than we would like it to be. These individuals who are resistant to love will not change, regardless of how long or how well you have tended the relationship. These are the relationships you need to set serious limits on or, sometimes, even end altogether.

The next chapter will show you how you can tell if it's time to curtail or end a relationship with someone who is resistant to even your most sincere and consistent efforts to love him or her into change.

6

Enough Is Enough: How to Set Limits That Help and Heal

Noel, Noel,
Noel, Noel.
May All My Enemies,
Go to hell.

~ Hilaire Belloc

The truth is that sometimes the other person will never, ever change. Most of us have such a person in our lives. So what do you do when you're stuck with a person who is stuck?

During a recent visit to her husband's parents, Daphne encountered the following helpful advice from her mother-in-law, Joyce.

"I don't mean to pry, dear, but that's really not your best look. Those pants make you look a little—hippy—you know? Oh well, I guess there isn't a lot of motivation to look your best when you're just home all day, is there?"

This was just the most recent in a long line of helpful comments from Joyce, whose career as an advice maven began fourteen years ago when Daphne and her husband, Mark, announced their engagement. Joyce pulled Mark aside to say, "Of course I'm happy for you, honey, but don't you think she's a little beneath you?" Despite Daphne's best efforts to extend numerous olive branches through the years, the relationship between Daphne and Joyce had just gone downhill from there.

Aaron had been Curtis's best friend since high school and had been Curtis's best man at his wedding. Aaron had always struggled with problem drinking. On and off since high school, Curtis had had to get Aaron out of trouble. Curtis had never felt that things were too out of control, though, and he had always been glad to be there to help Aaron when he needed it. During such times, Curtis would give his friend a shoulder to cry on, some strong coffee, and some stronger straight talk about how Aaron needed to pull himself together, and usually these interventions worked. Recently, though, Aaron's drinking had gotten increasingly out of control, and Curtis felt that his friendship with Aaron was causing him to lose too much time with his wife and three children. The last straw was when Aaron got a DUI and called Curtis at three in the morning to ask Curtis to bail him out of jail. Aaron had never been in trouble with the law before, and the whole situation left Curtis with a bad taste in his mouth. "I'm not sure how much longer I can do this for him—or even if I should. Aaron is starting to cut too much into my life, and at the same time I feel guilty even saying that. I mean, we've always been there for each other. Still, I'm just not sure I know if it's time to say, 'Enough is enough.' "

So far, we've been looking at how to create change in your problem relationships. But change is a two-way street, and sometimes you're the only one on the road. Assuming that you have tried the techniques we have examined so far in the book and have not met with success, then it's probably time to think about setting some limits.

Setting boundaries is often difficult for Christians because we place such a high value on compassion. But compassion without justice is not true Christian compassion. In fact, as we saw in chapter 2, compassion without justice can be downright pathological. (See pp. 22–24, "Was Jesus Codependent?")

Scripture shows us that limit setting is an absolutely acceptable practice, so long as it is done in the right spirit and at the right time. Jesus set limits when he refused to chase after the young rich man who would not sell his possessions and follow Jesus. Likewise, Jesus set very firm limits with the religious leaders, who tried to trip him up at every turn, and he taught his apostles to set limits when he instructed them to shake from their feet the dust of the towns that would not hear the truth of the gospel.

As I mentioned in an earlier chapter, Christ has even given us a format to follow in determining whether or not to set limits with a certain person.

First we are to try to reconcile with the other person ourselves. Failing this, we are to seek the help of an "elder," that is, a wise friend or pastor who can engage in informal mediation between the other person and us. If this does not work, then we are to seek professional help, perhaps from a professional mediator such as a counselor. If all of this fails, then we are to set limits on the relationship—or in some cases, end it altogether.

So "writing off" someone can be an acceptable option for Christians, but it is absolutely a last-resort method. Christianity places a premium on peace and unity within the community of believers.

Keeping this in mind, in this chapter we are going to carefully approach limit setting, beginning with a kind of examination of conscience. This leads up to setting what I like to call "semipermeable boundaries." Finally, I will give you the skills to decide when it is time to end a relationship.

Limit Setting: Examining Your Conscience

> Do not be rash to make new friends, and when they are made, do not be rash to drop them.
>
> ~ Diogenes Laertius

The first step in setting respectful limits with another person is to ask yourself several questions about the context in which you are setting the limits and the reasons you want to set them. As you saw in chapter 2, problems can arise when people are either too quick or too slow to draw the line when dealing with difficult relationships. The following four questions provide a kind of examination of conscience to help you decide whether or not it is time to put some distance between yourself and another person.

1. Is this truly an important issue, or am I getting upset over petty things?
2. Is it really time to set a limit, or am I just being impatient?
3. Have I sincerely tried to work through the P-E-A-C-E process, or am I just giving up because I lack the will or desire to heal the relationship?
4. If we have failed to solve the problem on our own, is there someone we can turn to for mediation? If so, have we sought the help of this person?

Let's take a closer look at each of these questions.

Is this truly an important issue, or am I getting upset over petty things?

In other words, is the problem you are concerned with really worth the effort it would take to change it? Or would it be better for you to view this situation as an opportunity to become more tolerant, mature, and open-minded—not to mention less petty—on your own?

I also asked you to examine this question in chapter 2. But assuming that you have failed in your efforts to change the problem, it is time to revisit this question, because it is quite possible that a peaceful future relationship hangs in the balance. Important issues that are appropriate for limit setting include the following.

The person in question is a threat to my physical safety. This ought to be a no-brainer. Obviously, if your physical safety is at stake, the rule is get out now and ask questions later. Period. You may be able to work on the relationship later—if you wish, if that is even an option. But for now, nothing is more important than establishing the distance you need to protect the gift of life and health that God has given you and over which he has made you a guardian.

Some faithful Catholics I know who were involved in abusive relationships of one kind or another objected to this logic, saying, "But Jesus suffered at the hands of others—why shouldn't I be expected to do the same?" I fear that some readers may be thinking the same thing. To you, I offer a word of caution. Remember that Jesus carefully chose when to suffer and when not to suffer. Sometimes, he intentionally avoided or even ran away from opportunities to suffer at the hands of others. When he did suffer, it was because the unique purpose of his life—the salvation of the world—required him to suffer, and even then, he asked the Father to, if there was any other way, "let this cup [of suffering] pass." Jesus did not view the threat of physical harm lightly. Neither should you. If you believe that it is your job to suffer physical harm for the sake of a spouse, a child, or another important person in your life, I strongly urge you to speak to your pastor or a faithful Christian counselor, who can help you properly discern the true purpose of your life and the most respectful ways to fulfill that purpose.

The person in question acts or speaks in a consistently demeaning way to me and is unsympathetic to my direct and honest efforts to correct him. This issue is similar to that of physical violence. Granted, from time to time, and sometimes consistently, everybody offends someone else, often without realizing it. But if a person is consistently treating you in an offensive or demeaning way and that person ignores or dismisses your objections to his or her behavior, most likely this is the kind of toxic person that you can justifiably rid yourself of. These kinds of people include those who, when you tell them that they are being cruel, insist that they were "just joking" and that you are "too sensitive."

It really doesn't matter if the person intends to offend you or not. If I offend you, the loving thing for me to do is to first try to explain myself in a way that is satisfying to you—or, failing that, to try my absolute best to not do that thing again. Alternatively, if I refuse to act in a loving and respectful way toward you, most likely you would be better off without me.

This person is preventing me from becoming the person I believe God is calling me to be. You, like every one of us, were put on this earth to fulfill a purpose. When other people stand in the way of your living out the life or completing the tasks you sincerely believe that God has placed on your heart, your first obligation is to try to negotiate with them. They are, after all, entitled to express their concerns over your choices and to ask you to seek ways to fulfill your dreams, goals, and spiritual ideals in a manner that is respectful to them as well.

But if those same people refuse to negotiate with you, if they actively and consistently attempt to undermine your efforts to become a more complete and more fulfilled person, or if they intentionally throw barriers in your way, then your duty to God—the one who gave you your mission—obliges you to distance yourself from those people.

No one may ever stand between you and the person God is calling you to be. If they do, and if the P-E-A-C-E process fails to resolve that, then it may be appropriate to set limits on your relationship with those people.

This person seeks to stop me from achieving something (be it a spiritual, emotional, relational, or material goal) that is important to my sense of well-being. Perhaps the person with whom you are in conflict does not hit you or demean you. Perhaps she doesn't even stand between you and the person God wants you to be. But let's say that she refuses to help you acquire the things—be they emotional, spiritual, relational, or even material things—that you believe are essential to your sense of well-being. If this is true, and assuming the P-E-A-C-E process has failed to resolve the problem, it is time to consider setting some limits on the relationship.

I would add only two qualifiers here. A person is entitled to express concerns over the things that you say you need to be satisfied in the life God gave you. She even has the right to disagree with you, to point out the reasons why she thinks those things may be unhealthy or undesirable. However, if in spite of those *respectful* objections you continue to insist that what you want is truly necessary for your general sense of well-being, then she is obliged to support you in your pursuit of it. If she continues to stand in your way or demeans you for needing what you need, then it may be appropriate to set limits on this relationship.

This person is a time bandit. Certain people have a sense of entitlement when it comes to your time and energy. While you should give as much as you can to others as long as it does not jeopardize your primary relationships, you are not obliged to give more than that. Even so, some employers, friends, and family members act as if every moment you have belongs to them. Talk to this person first, but assuming that this fails and that he continues to demand more than his reasonable share of the time you have left after fulfilling God-given primary obligations, then this may well be an issue that requires you to set limits on your relationship.

This person wants me to work harder at solving the problem than he or she works. Some people want you to solve their problems or support them while they never lift a finger to help themselves. Offering to help such a person is not really helping; it is enabling him or her to continue to function in a less than healthy way.

It is one thing to stand by someone who is sincerely struggling to overcome his or her problems. It is quite another thing for him to expect you to do all the work while he hangs back and watches. If this is the case, then it may be time to set some very firm limits on this relationship.

The preceding criteria may help you determine if an issue is really serious enough to require you to set limits on a relationship. Here are some examples of things that, generally speaking, do not require you to set limits on a relationship, but rather present an opportunity for you to overcome your own pettiness.

- Differences in preference: He likes country music; you like classical.
- Differences in method: She completes the tasks you ask her to do to a satisfactory level, but she doesn't do it the *way* you wanted her to do it.
- True differences of opinion: He thinks it is better to work before you play; you think it is better to play before you work.

Such issues may be fair game for the P-E-A-C-E process, but for the most part, they are not worth making a serious fuss over. If the other person continues to feel strongly about having his way in one of these situations, my recommendation is that you defer to him and save the "points" you earn for an issue that really matters to you. (Remember the emotional bank account discussion in chapter 5.)

Now let's examine the second question.

Is it really time to set a limit, or am I just being impatient?

Let's say that you have decided that you are not being petty and that the issue at hand really is serious enough to warrant setting limits. In that case, it might be helpful to ask a second question: Is it really time to set a limit, or am I just being impatient?

I recently counseled a couple who had made great strides in marital therapy. Even though they still had a way to go, both the husband and the wife consistently agreed that things were getting better all the time. Imagine my surprise, then, when the young man came to the next session and announced that it would be his last meeting. He had decided to file for divorce.

I asked him what was wrong. Hadn't he said that things were improving? Had I missed something? He told me that although the situation had gotten significantly better, he felt discouraged that there was still work left to do, and he was tired of working on it. It was taking too much time and energy to repair the marriage, and he just didn't want to do it anymore.

This is a good example of what I am talking about. If someone is not trying to change at all or is constantly dragging his feet when enacting the changes you and he have agreed upon, then it is absolutely appropriate to set limits on, or even end, your relationship with that person. However, if the other person is making a sincere effort to enact the changes that need to be made but it is just taking longer than you would like, then, dear reader, you need to get over yourself. Our Christian duty to others does not require us to be doormats, but it does require us to stand by others as long as they are sincerely struggling to do what is right—even when it takes longer than we might like. If you want to set limits on a relationship, make sure it is because the situation calls for it and not just because you are tired of working on it.

Have I sincerely tried to work through the P-E-A-C-E process, or am I just giving up because I lack the will or desire to heal the relationship?

This is similar to the last point. Let's say that you go through the P-E-A-C-E process once with someone, but it doesn't work all that well. At this point, many people are tempted to say, "Well, then. That's it for you!" and write off the other person.

The correct way to handle this problem is to assume that you may have missed something the first time through the process. If the other person negotiated with you in what appeared to be good faith, then you need to give her the benefit of the doubt and try again.

But if the other person refuses to continue to work with you on the problem, denies that there is a problem, or agrees to your plan "just to shut you up" but has no intention of following through, then you may be absolutely within your rights to begin setting limits on the relationship. There is just one more question to examine before you make your final decision.

If we have failed to solve this problem on our own, is there someone we can turn to for mediation? If so, have we sought the help of this person?

You can't solve every problem on your own. Sometimes it is wise to seek the help of a friend or a trained professional. If you and the person you are in conflict with are unable to resolve your differences on your own, Scripture instructs you to try to find someone to mediate your dispute. Often, the mediator can be a mutually respected friend or coworker, a pastor, or even a counselor. If such a person is available, you are obliged to make use of his or her services whenever possible before limiting or terminating your relationship.

Sometimes, however, this is simply not possible, especially when neither of you can agree on a mediator to help you resolve the dispute fairly.

Or, occasionally, the other person is unwilling to avail himself of the help of a third party. If either of these cases is true, or if mediation by a third party is unsuccessful, then it is completely acceptable to begin setting some limits on the relationship.

The First Step: Setting Partial Limits

Once you have decided to set limits on a relationship, it is best to try to save some part of that relationship whenever possible. Just because a certain friend of mine is irresponsible, I may not have to write him off entirely. Instead, I may no longer ask for his help on certain projects. I may still call him when I am looking for someone to goof around with, but I will no longer include him in the important events in my life—because he has shown me that he can't be trusted and that he is unwilling to work with me. In this way, setting partial limits on the relationship will protect my sanity while still allowing me to enjoy the healthy parts of my relationship with my friend.

The case that began this chapter is a good example of this principle. Even though Joyce was a lousy mother-in-law who did not care to get along with Daphne except on the most superficial level, Joyce was wonderful to Daphne's children. She loved being a grandmother and doted on the children—and they loved Joyce very much. Because of this, Daphne felt it would be unreasonable to cut Joyce out of her life completely. True, Daphne did not invite Joyce to her home very often, nor did Daphne and her husband stay long when visiting Joyce. Instead, since Joyce couldn't seem to stop herself from making obnoxious comments to Daphne thirty minutes or so into a visit, Daphne and her husband occasionally "popped in" for a brief visit and then left before things could turn sour. Even so, they allowed Joyce to baby-sit their children—something that Joyce both enjoyed and was good at. They stayed engaged with Joyce to this extent, despite Daphne's constant temptation to cut Joyce out of her life entirely. As Daphne put it, "I decided that I am going to be a big girl and, for the sake of my kids, keep up a minimal relationship with Joyce. I am never going to be that woman's best friend, and frankly, I don't even want to try. It just isn't worth it anymore. But I will at the very least be civil to her, because she is kind to my children and she loves my husband very much. At least we have that in common."

As you can see, setting partial limits is an attempt to avoid throwing out the proverbial baby with the bathwater. By setting partial limits, we enable ourselves to enjoy the positive aspects of our relationship with another person while protecting ourselves from that person's craziness. Some people have an all-or-nothing attitude toward their relationships with others. These individuals might say, "Either I can trust you totally or I don't have time for you in my life." While I sympathize with this sentiment, it is not realistic. Everyone has a personality trait that is unappealing to someone else. If we went around running people out of our lives because of their tics—obnoxious though they may be—we would inevitably come to lead long, lonely lives. Generally speaking, if there are some redeemable parts of a relationship, however small, it is not a bad idea to try to hold on to the relationship while taking whatever steps necessary to insulate ourselves from the more toxic aspects of the other individual's personality. In order to do this, we need to become comfortable with the idea of setting partial limits.

Two types of limits fit into this category: limits on action and limits on tolerance.

Limits on action

These limits involve our refusal to participate in certain offensive activities that the other person might ask us to do.

Brenda, a telephone client of mine, called me to work on issues in her relationship with Letty, her mother. Brenda loved her mother dearly and because of this felt terribly guilty whenever she refused one of Letty's requests. In fact, she had a hard time saying no to anyone, and this was doubly true where her mother was concerned. The problem was that Brenda's mother did not like to do things for herself. She would frequently call Brenda to ask her to pick up things at the grocery store or run other errands for her. Brenda's mom was physically capable of doing these chores; in fact, she worked a full-time job, drove a car, and was quite healthy. The ironic thing was that Letty lived across the street from the grocery store, while Brenda had to drive across town to go to the market. This did not stop Letty from asking Brenda if she would mind picking up "a few things from the market" because Letty was tired after work.

Brenda said that she really didn't mind this, except that the frequent requests were preventing her from getting her own work done, which was in turn cutting into her time with her husband and children. As Brenda put it, "My mom has always been great to me, but Dad used to take care of her like this. Ever since he's been sick, she has been relying on me to take his place. I don't have the heart to tell her I can't do it—she's so upset about my dad—but I'm honestly starting to get physically ill from all the stress."

Over the next few sessions, what helped Brenda most was learning the difference between reasonable and unreasonable requests. She could still be generous in fulfilling the reasonable requests—those that were respectful of her own work and relationships and with which her mother really needed help. But she could also refuse the unreasonable ones—those that were not respectful of her own work and relationships and that her mother could more easily do for herself.

The biggest fear Brenda had was that in order to say no to her mother's requests, she would have to cut off her relationship with her mom entirely. Once Brenda understood that she could say no to certain things her mother asked her to do but still allow herself to enjoy the healthy parts of their relationship, she found that, emotionally speaking, she was in a much better place.

Some readers may be tempted to dismiss this point I'm making as obvious—*of course* we can set these kinds of limits. But all of us, at one time or another, have been tempted to end a relationship because a person has one obnoxious trait. How much better would it be if we could simply insulate ourselves from the unhealthy part of the relationship while still enjoying the more pleasant parts? This is not always possible, but when it is, it is advisable. Not only does it preserve the relationship, but it also requires us to foster the maturity and personal strength needed to relate to other people lovingly in spite of all their faults. If someone ever asks you to do something that violates your principles, steals too much time from your most important commitments, or causes you to work harder to take care of that person than he or she is working (assuming that she is healthy and able to help herself), then you would do well to set a limit on action.

Limits on tolerance

These limits involve our refusal to endure certain kinds of treatment from another person.

Lane and Sam had been married for ten years, and Sam wasn't sure they were going to make it to their eleventh anniversary. Sam was able to point to many times when he and Lane had enjoyed each other's company and had gotten along well. The problem was that when they got into disagreements, Lane would quickly lose her cool. Sam said that even when the conversation was only mildly tense, Lane would immediately threaten divorce, storm out of the house, or ignore Sam for days until she calmed down, at which point she would emerge from her mood as if nothing had happened. When I asked her if she agreed with Sam's assessment, she admitted that his description of her behavior was correct, but she refused to accept that she had a problem. "He knew what I was like when he married me, and I resent him trying to change me now." In fact, Sam had tried using the P-E-A-C-E process with Lane, but she had simply refused, saying, "I don't have the problem; you do."

Sam was ready to give up on the marriage, but I asked him if it would be worth it to try to set some limits and see what results that brought. He was game, so I suggested that if his wife lost her cool, then he was to simply say, "Lane, I love you and I want to hear what you have to say, but I can't listen to you unless you are willing to calm down and talk to me respectfully. Can you do that, or do we need to take a break?"

He was not to continue the discussion with Lane unless she agreed to calm down. If she refused, he was to repeat his request. If this was unsuccessful, he was to ignore her (or if she pushed too hard, I instructed him to go someplace where he could be alone—either in the house or elsewhere) until she calmed down or left the room herself. Then, when she was calmer, he was to ask her if she was ready to talk and to remind her that he really did want to hear what she had to say as long as they could manage to work together and be calm. The rest was up to her.

The weeks that followed were an interesting time for Sam. He had never stood up to Lane's anger so respectfully and consistently before. Usually, he either started screaming at her or withdrew into himself in the hopes that all the fuss would simply blow over. At first, Lane continued to act in the same manner in which she had always acted, but even so, Sam was relieved because he had never felt so in control of himself during these arguments. In session, he told me that after a few weeks he wasn't intimidated by her anger any longer. He said he knew that as long as he reassured her that he wanted to listen to her, he had nothing to feel guilty about. Interestingly, once Lane realized that Sam was not going to be pulled into the old game and that he really was willing to hear her out (and was not just telling her that to get her off his back), she began dealing with him in a more reasonable way. It was slow going, but she finally agreed to rejoin therapy with her husband and commit to learning how to problem solve instead of fight.

Sometimes we need to be willing to set boundaries in our relationships. This is usually the case when someone refuses to admit that he or she is acting in an offensive way. Perhaps this person says that he is "just joking" and tells you to lighten up. Or perhaps he tells you that your concern with his treatment of you is your problem, not his.

When this happens, you must draw a line in the sand. Often my clients will complain that the people in their lives do not respect the limits they set—especially when it comes to the way they are being treated by a spouse, an adult child, or an alleged friend. Usually, the reason my clients' boundaries are not being respected is that they are asking the offending person's permission to set the limit.

Margery, a forty-two-year-old client, had begun working out of the home for the first time in her life, and she enjoyed her work as a veterinarian assistant. Unfortunately, her husband was less than supportive of this effort; in fact, he felt downright threatened by it. In response to Margery's taking the job, he complained, whined, pouted, argued, and did everything else he could think of to wear her down. While I always try to keep an open mind about such things, it was clear to me that this man did not have a legitimate complaint. His wife's work was not taking anything away from the relationship—they worked similar hours and were gone from home at essentially the same time. Margery's work did not negatively affect any of her usual duties around the house. They had cleaning help and Margery continued to cook all of the meals. The only reason her husband objected to her working out of the home—and he admitted as much—was because "I like to know where she is and what she's doing, and I can't do that if she's not home." Clearly, his was not a reasonable position.

The pressure was taking its toll on Margery. While her husband was at no time abusive in any way, there was constant tension in the house, and Margery was a woman who built her life around avoiding tension. She complained to me one day, "I think I'm going to have to quit. He just won't let up. No matter how I try to explain it to him, he won't accept the limit I'm trying to set around work (that is, that her working was not negotiable)."

Margery was trying to get her husband to accept her limit, to understand it, to appreciate it, and to approve of it. This was never going to happen. The good news is that it is not necessary for another person to understand and approve of a boundary you set; he just has to live by it (and you have to consistently enforce it).

If I tell you that if you punch me in the nose, I will have you arrested, then my having you arrested is not dependent upon your saying to me, "Yes, Greg. That sounds like a very good idea." Rather, your arrest is an automatic consequence of your punching me in the nose, whether you like it or not. When someone treats you in a manner that you find demeaning or cruel, first use the problem-solving strategies outlined in this book to try to discover the true intention behind the behavior and arrive at some possible solutions. Failing that, though, you are well within your rights to say, "If you want to be in a relationship with me, you need to stop treating me like that, because if you don't, I will (spend less time with you, refuse to work with you on this project, ask you to leave, stop thinking of you as a friend, etc.)."

If the other person persists in the offensive behavior, then the consequence (usually some kind of distance in the relationship) should be enforced immediately. Earlier I gave the example of Daphne and her mother-in-law, Joyce. Joyce refused to acknowledge that she was being offensive in any way: "Don't be so sensitive, dear. I'm only trying to offer some constructive criticism." Daphne and Mark decided that they didn't want to write off Joyce entirely, mostly for the sake of the grandchildren, but they did need to set some limits on their own relationship with Joyce for Daphne's sake. So Mark and Daphne agreed that as long as Joyce was being at least moderately civil to Daphne, they would continue the visit (or phone conversation) they were having, but as soon as things turned sour, they would find some excuse—no matter how lame it was—to leave. They did this even without telling Joyce, since they felt it wouldn't do any good anyway. They simply decided to be respectful as long as Joyce did the same, and when she wasn't, they let their absence (their limit) do the talking for them.

Joyce was livid the first time Mark and Daphne did this. She told Daphne that she was being ridiculous. She accused Mark of betraying her, but Mark and Daphne stood fast. In response to her complaints, both Mark and Daphne—at different times—explained that they wanted Joyce to be a part of their life, but not if she insisted on acting "that way." The couple did not ask for an apology—that would have simply been wasting their breath—but neither did they stay away from Joyce until she promised to change. They continued to call and visit, but as soon as Joyce acted in a way that was offensive, they ended the visit. By consistently doing this, Joyce understood two things. First, she saw that Daphne and Mark were not just writing her off. Their continued visits and conversations let Joyce know that they weren't just telling her what she wanted to hear when they said they wanted her to be a part of their life. At the same time, their hasty but respectful and non-argumentative exits sent a clear message that they were unwilling to submit themselves to Joyce's none-too-constructive criticisms. In time, Mark and Daphne were genuinely surprised to see Joyce mending her ways. It took about six months for the complete effect to take hold, but they noticed a significant improvement within the first few weeks. Joyce was trying harder, albeit reluctantly, because having a relationship with her son, his wife, and her grandchildren was important to her. She did not want to be the cause of a permanent rift, and even though, if asked, she would have continued to argue that she was not doing anything wrong, she changed her behavior because Mark and Daphne made it clear that if she wanted to be in a relationship with them, she needed to treat them with respect.

This is the essence of setting what I call "a limit on tolerance": being willing to say, "If you want to have a relationship with me, you need to act in a certain way toward me. If you don't, I will withdraw from you." When all other attempts to change the behavior have failed, you need to be willing to set this limit automatically and consistently, whether the offending person likes it or not. By doing it the way I've described—that is, by not cutting off the relationship entirely, but rather putting immediate distance between you and the other person when he or she steps out of line—you let the other person know that you are willing to be reasonable (by not terminating the relationship), but that you are also not willing to be a doormat. The other person may not always like your limit, but if he wants to be in a relationship with you, he will respect it. If he doesn't, then it will be time to sever the relationship entirely.

The Last Step: What to Do When It's Time to End the Relationship

God is a merciful God. God constantly seeks ways to reach out to us, to love us, to teach us, and to enter into a deep, personal relationship with us. Still, even the Lord has his limits. Scripture says, "You are my friends, *if you keep my commands*" (John 15:14, italics mine). In a sense, this is the scriptural basis for the limits on tolerance discussed in this chapter. Jesus was saying, "I love you more than you could ever know, but if you want to be in a relationship with me, then you need to act in a certain way toward me. If you do not, I will withdraw from you, and if you continue to act offensively toward me, you may lose my friendship entirely."

Losing God's friendship is a terrible thing. For us, it means hell. For God, it means losing a dear son or daughter. Because this loss is so terrible, God does not suffer it lightly. In fact, God went so far as to send his Son to procure our salvation in an effort to decrease the chances of losing even one of his children. God uses every reasonable means to salvage even the smallest bit of a relationship with the people he loves so dearly. Sadly, though, a person sometimes chooses, freely and consistently, not to befriend God. The resulting loss of divine friendship, though mourned, cannot be helped.

In the same way, we must do everything we can to maintain a relationship with the offensive people in our life. Still, there will be times when a person consistently chooses to act in a way that makes friendship—or even civility—impossible. Under these circumstances, and with great sadness, we have no choice but to respond the same way our heavenly Father responds when his friendship is spurned. We must withdraw ourselves from that person, perhaps permanently.

The decision to end a relationship, any relationship, should not be taken lightly. In order to maintain your dignity and satisfy your conscience, follow one rule of thumb for ending a relationship: Never intentionally alienate people, but don't stop them from alienating themselves.

If you consider yourself to be God's friend, then driving someone away with insults, accusations, cruelty, or your own pettiness is inexcusable. It is, however, completely acceptable to set parameters that define your relationship—to, in effect, say to a person, "Being in a relationship with me requires a certain level of behavior on your part. If you can manage that, then you can be my friend/husband/wife/son/daughter/sister/brother. If you cannot, I won't act offensively toward you, but I won't stand between you and the door either."

Bethany had been dating Martin for almost two years. They had had many good times together, and in many ways Bethany felt that Martin was the man she wanted to spend the rest of her life with.

Unfortunately, Martin had a very cruel sense of humor. He enjoyed making fun of people, often in front of them, even in public, and he did not spare Bethany his barbs. More times than she could count, he would say things to her in public that she felt were demeaning to her. He would comment on her looks, her intelligence, her mistakes—everything was fair game as far as Martin was concerned, and any time was the right time to exploit a person's flaws for the sake of a laugh.

When Bethany complained, Martin's response varied from offering a half-hearted get-off-my-back apology to dismissing her concerns, saying that she was "too insecure" and "had to learn to lighten up." He would insist that he didn't treat her any differently than he treated anyone else and that it "didn't mean anything." It was just his sense of humor. Didn't she like his sense of humor? His friends seemed to.

Martin was right in one sense. He didn't treat Bethany any differently than he treated any of his friends. He was an equal-opportunity humiliator. For a long time, this fact made Bethany unsure of whether her complaints were legitimate. Maybe she was just too uptight. Martin's friends didn't seem to mind his treatment, so why should she? And besides, wasn't the rest of their relationship so good? Wasn't Martin capable of remarkable sweetness too?

Nevertheless, Bethany's discomfort with Martin's sense of "humor" simply increased as time passed. She tried using many of the strategies described in this book, and then some, to address the issue with Martin. None of them worked, largely because he refused to admit that he was doing something offensive. When the healthy ways of trying to fix the problem failed, Bethany tried some unhealthy ones just for good measure. Sometimes she yelled at him and called him names; sometimes she pouted or cried; once she even tried to give him a taste of his own medicine by making fun of him in public, but it backfired. She ended up feeling small for doing something so beneath her, and he just teased her more fiercely.

In counseling, Bethany finally decided that she needed to set a limit of tolerance. She hoped that setting a clear boundary and showing Martin how serious this issue really was to her would create the change she wanted.

One evening, she said to him, "I love you so much, but if you want to be in a relationship with me, you need to stop telling jokes at my expense." He pooh-poohed her as usual, but this time she had a respectful and firm response. "The next time you make me uncomfortable like that, I'll leave you there. And unless you show me that you are willing to change, that will be the end of our relationship."

Even though she said this sincerely and meant every word, she wasn't sure Martin was convinced. It wouldn't be long before she had a chance to test it out. Two days later, they attended a dinner party at a friend's home. At first, things went very well, but as the evening wore on, Martin reverted to his repertoire of put-downs and "jokes" at Bethany's expense. She didn't say anything. Instead, she excused herself as if she was going to use the restroom. She used her cell phone to call a cab, and twenty minutes later she left the party, saying that she was sorry, but she didn't feel well (which was true, at least in the emotional sense). When the other people at the party asked her why she had called a cab, Bethany just said that she didn't want to spoil anyone else's fun and she preferred to go home alone. While it was clear to everyone what the problem was, Bethany did not make a scene in any way. She conducted herself with as much dignity as possible, even though—as she told me later—she was trembling inside and cried all the way home in the cab.

Later that night, Martin appeared on her doorstep demanding an explanation. He was furious. He told her that she had humiliated him in front of his friends and had made herself "look like a baby." Bethany reminded Martin that she only did what she told him she was going to do and if he wanted to continue the relationship with her, he would have to change his behavior. Incensed, Martin refused, saying, "I am who I am, and if you can't respect that, then I don't want anything to do with you!"

Painful as it was, Bethany told Martin that if he truly felt that way, he had better leave. At the door, she told him again that she loved him and that if he changed his mind, he should call her, but if he couldn't, then it would be better if they didn't see each other anymore. He left. That was the end of their relationship.

Bethany told me later that it was one of the hardest things she had ever had to do, but she said that at the same time she felt proud of herself. She didn't do anything demeaning to herself that night. She didn't bring herself down to Martin's level, and she didn't pout or act defensive or accusatory. She simply set her limit and stuck to it. She gave him a choice. She wanted him to choose her, but she gave him the freedom to walk out of her life if he was unwilling to do what it took to have a relationship with her. Her choice took courage, and even though the breakup was painful, she had conducted herself with strength and grace.

Whenever possible, you should do what you can to salvage at least some portion of a relationship. But when a person refuses to act in a way that is consistent with your friendship or contributes to your well-being, it is best to set some kind of limit. If that person really loves you, in the Christian sense of being willing to work for your good, then that person, however reluctantly, will eventually come to accept your limit. If, however, that person values his own comfort level, pride, or manner of doing things more than your friendship, then you are better off without him. Such a person is a false friend, whose friendship comes at the cost of both your self-esteem and the dignity God grants you as a child of God.

With such a person, you do not need to do anything offensive to get him out of your life. No screaming, begging, whining, pouting, accusing, belittling, nagging, guilting, or name-calling is necessary. All you have to do is set a reasonable limit and then leave it up to him. By setting limits in this manner, you protect your own Christian dignity. Even if you must eventually grieve the loss of a friend, you will know that you have done everything within your power to salvage at least some part of the relationship and that the responsibility for ending it rests upon the other person's shoulders.

LIMIT SETTING: AN EXERCISE

Identify someone who you feel is unwilling to work with you to resolve a particular problem. Write down the name of the person and the offensive behavior.

Try using the P-E-A-C-E process if you haven't already. If you have tried those strategies and have failed, go on to the next step.

Come up with a limit on action or on tolerance. How could you use a limit on action or a limit on tolerance to force change in the relationship? Write down your answer.

Remember, you cannot ask permission to set a limit. A limit is a line you draw in the sand, something you enforce regardless of the other person's reaction. A good limit requires some consequence as well. This consequence is not a threat or an attempt to bully another into submission. It is simply the way you will pull back from the person if he or she continues to ignore your limit. Complete the following statement in order to know what to say to someone when you set a limit with him or her:

"I want to have a peaceful relationship with you, but in order to do that, I need you to (state the limit). If you don't do this, I will (not work with you on a particular project/visit you less/end our relationship/refuse to talk to you until you calm down—state your consequence).

Once you have set your limit, consistently enforce it for at least a month before thinking of ending the relationship. Is the person respecting your limit? Even if she is accepting it grudgingly, you are succeeding. Remember, others are entitled to their opinions of your limit, but that doesn't mean you have to change it. On the other hand, if that person continues to offend you and refuses to accept your limit, it is probably time to end the relationship. This may be a sad option to consider, but when you have tried everything else it is sometimes the only option that remains. Have the courage to do what needs to be done to maintain your own God-given dignity and do not let the grief you feel over losing a friend stop you from enforcing the limit. Remember: God grieves for every soul that is estranged from him too, but he does not befriend those who do not desire his friendship.

Finally, remember the rule of thumb: Never alienate people, but don't stop them from alienating themselves.

One More Story

Before you begin the next chapter of the book, which will give you specific examples of how to apply these strategies to the problem relationships in your life, read the following story. Perhaps it will help you see how setting respectful limits can clarify even the most confusing situation.

Nicole had been married for ten difficult years when she and her husband, Bill, finally decided to file for divorce. They had separated twice before, only to get back together because they missed each other and they felt guilty about the idea of divorce. Nicole confessed to me that she was having those old feelings again, feelings that consisted of sexual longing, nostalgia for the good times she and her husband had had together, and guilt about the moral implications of divorce. She told me that Bill was feeling the same way.

Being a marriage counselor, I admitted my own bias to Nicole, which is that one should preserve any marriage worth preserving, and this prompted her question: How do you know whether a marriage is worth saving or not?

In my marriage book, *For Better...Forever!* I assert that the purpose of two people uniting in Christian marriage is to help each other become the person God wants him or her to be "when he or she grows up." I explained to Nicole that rather than rely on her feelings to tell her whether she and Bill should reunite or not, she should first identify what kind of person God was calling her to become and then ask Bill if he could support her in that mission. In the course of our conversations, Nicole decided that God was calling her to become a more peaceful and stronger person. She also felt led to return to school to prepare for a career change. I then asked her what she would need from Bill in order to feel supported in these goals. She told me that in order to feel more peaceful and to stay in the marriage, she needed Bill to work on his temper. In order to feel stronger and to stay in her marriage, she needed Bill to stop going out with his friends every night after work and to spend time with her. This would help her confidence, because presently she felt as if she wasn't worth much if even her husband couldn't make time for her. Finally, to pursue the call she felt God was giving her and to stay in the marriage, she needed Bill to encourage her about school and the career-change idea. Previously, he had strongly objected to her plans, saying they were silly.

Once she had identified these criteria, I instructed Nicole to call Bill and set up a meeting. When they got together, she was to say to Bill, "I would really like to save this marriage, but in order for this to work, I need three things from you. I need you to be willing to work on your temper, I need you to spend less time with your friends and more time with me, and I need you to support me in my plans to return to school and change careers." After delivering this message, she was to be quiet and listen to his answer.

Three days later she called me to tell me the result of her conversation with Bill. "Well, we had our meeting, and his answers to my three questions were 'I don't have a problem with my temper,' 'I don't want to spend less time with my friends,' and 'I don't think I could do that.'" These answers, of course, led Nicole to a clear sense of what she needed to do next. Six months later, with much sadness, they finalized their divorce.

By setting the kind of limit that she did, Nicole maintained her dignity and was able to discern what path to follow. She was not rude to Bill, and she did nothing to alienate him—in fact, she did quite the opposite. All she did was tell him what it would take, based on a desire to be faithful to God's call in her life, for her to be willing to work on the relationship with him. Then she left the choice to Bill. Bill alienated himself with his answer.

Setting limits is always difficult, especially when it leads to the end of a relationship. Fortunately in most cases, setting limits yields more hopeful results. If you are struggling with setting limits in your life or would like additional tips for and support in setting respectful boundaries, I invite you to call me at the Pastoral Solutions Institute at (740) 266-6461.

Now that we've covered the many different ways you can create change or, when necessary, set limits in your problem relationships, we'll look at some specific examples of how to use these techniques to bring greater peace to your life.

7

The Enemy Within: How to Love the You That God Loves

Self-respect. That cornerstone of all virtue.

~ Sir John Herschel

Love your neighbor as yourself.

~ Matthew 19:19

Jesus tells us that we are to love our neighbors as we love ourselves. Unfortunately, many people do not have a healthy understanding of what it means to love themselves, and so spouses, children, coworkers, and friends suffer the consequences.

Henry had been married to his second wife, Liz, for ten years when they came to me for marriage counseling. Soon into our sessions, however, it became apparent that it was not so much their marriage that was suffering as Henry.

Henry drove himself hard. He criticized himself mercilessly for the mistakes he made. He was very sensitive to what others thought of him, and he tried hard to appear at all times as if he had everything under control.

Henry's lack of compassion for himself spilled over into his relationships with Liz and her daughter. In fact, his highly critical manner had already caused an almost irreparable rift with his son from Henry's previous marriage. Henry was not hostile, but he was extremely sensitive, to the point that if anyone said anything even remotely critical, he became either seriously depressed or bitterly defensive, depending on the day.

I began counseling Henry individually. During one session he confessed to me, "I can't cut them [his wife and children] any slack because I can't cut myself a break. Almost everything I do I feel like I screw up somehow, or like I'm not good enough. It's no wonder they don't like me. Hell, I don't even like me."

Even though Henry's case of self-hatred was more serious than most, we can all identify with him to some degree. Each one of us has at least one habit or one personality trait that we are ashamed of and wish we could overcome—or at least pretend doesn't exist.

And yet, there it stays. First this problem behavior or habit alienates us from ourselves by causing us to feel incompetent, foolish, and ashamed. Then the problem alienates us from others, either because the behavior itself is offensive or because we treat others' faults with the same unforgiving anger we unleash on ourselves.

Judith, a phone client, called because she felt that she was failing as a mom. The mother of three (ages eight, six, and four), she felt tired and overwhelmed much of the time. "I was an only child, so I spent a lot of time by myself reading and playing imaginary games. My kids aren't nearly as good at entertaining themselves. They'll play for a few minutes and then start bickering among themselves and want me to intervene. I know that's normal kid stuff, but because I never had to deal with that growing up, I don't know how to handle it. And then I start picking on myself because I lose my patience with the kids. I sit there after screaming at them and criticize myself for not being able to handle it like the books say I should. And that just makes it worse. Getting angry at myself puts me even more on edge with the kids, which makes me yell more...It's a vicious circle."

Although it seems natural to confront our failings and personal limitations with anger, for the most part this is exactly the wrong thing to do. I do not mean to suggest that guilt has no place, but it must play a limited role in our life if it is to remain healthy.

Understanding What Guilt Really Is

When we experience any kind of physical injury, the pain that results is like an alarm that is triggered, telling us to tend to the wound. In the same way, healthy guilt is the alarm that goes off after we injure our souls. It is the early warning signal that lets us know when we are doing something that is not in our best interest and tells us that we would do well to change our behavior.

Unfortunately, sometimes guilt, like pain, hangs around longer than is useful. Guilt alerts us to the problem, but after we have gotten the message, guilt sometimes decides to stick around and have a little fun with us instead of decreasing as it should. When this happens, we become paralyzed to do anything about our faults. In fact, as in Judith's case, this kind of guilt actually makes it harder for us to solve our problems. In effect, we end up spending so much energy feeling guilty that we don't have any energy left to change.

"But we're Christians," you might say (only half in jest). "We're supposed to feel guilty about everything!" Actually, this misperception is one of my pet peeves. (You know my motto: If you're going to have a pet, a peeve is the pet to get!) People, even faithful Christian people, believe that feeling guilty is part of being Christian. Well, it is, as long as you are referring to healthy guilt, which, of course, is just part of being human. Healthy guilt is a necessary part of growing in the virtues that make us truly human. We fail our ideals, we feel guilty. We strive to overcome the problem, the guilt goes away. But if you are referring to unhealthy guilt, then chances are you are talking about something the church actually condemns as a sin—the sin of scrupulosity.

Unhealthy guilt is something Satan uses to sap our energy so that we cannot change. Scrupulosity makes us feel guilty when we have no reason to feel guilty, and it makes us feel guilty longer than necessary even when we have done something wrong. Scrupulosity puts us beyond the reach of God's mercy (because it makes us believe that we don't deserve it), and it separates us from the grace we need to actually reform our lives (because it makes us believe that there is no hope for us). That is why the church tells us that pathological guilt (or what the church calls scrupulosity) is sinful.

Now, at the other end of the scale are those individuals who seem to love themselves a little too much. Such people think that they never do anything wrong, that if there is a problem, the responsibility (as well as any blame) lies not with them but with someone else. This is not love. This is the sin of pride. To truly love oneself means striking a balance between prideful self-aggrandizement and scrupulosity.

When we fail to live up to our own ideals or when we do something to offend or betray the trust of the ones we love, we are right to challenge our pride and accept the legitimate/healthy guilt that accompanies our offense. If that guilt then motivates us to make a real change in our lives (or at least come up with a workable plan to do so), then we have nothing left to feel guilty about. If, however, the guilt plagues and paralyzes us or if we fail to make a plan to change our life in spite of the guilt we feel, that is a matter for the confessional and, possibly, a counselor.

Moving On

Having experienced the loving correction of the Holy Spirit, that is, the healthy guilt that results from our offense, we are then obliged to do something about the personality trait or behavior that makes us feel guilty. But if beating ourselves up about the problem is not an acceptable practice for any good Christian, what is?

The best way to respond to our failings is by using a variation on the P-E-A-C-E process that we discussed earlier. This version of the P-E-A-C-E process has four steps.

1. Assess the positive intention or need behind the offense.
2. Brainstorm more respectful and efficient ways to meet that intention or need.
3. Develop a plan for using those more respectful and efficient methods.
4. Evaluate the plan and make improvements.

Let's examine each of these steps to learn how to experience greater love for ourselves and respectfully challenge our shortcomings.

Assess the positive intention or need behind the offense.

Even though we have already discussed how to do this, I find that it is always easier to apply techniques to other people than it is to apply them to myself. That's why I would like to take a minute to talk about how you can find the positive intention behind your own offensive behaviors.

First of all, just allowing yourself to believe that a positive intention is behind the obnoxious, offensive, sinful, or destructive things you do is a very freeing experience. No, it doesn't let you off the hook. And, no, it doesn't mean that you can avoid confessing personal shortcomings to God or to others in order to receive forgiveness for those stupid things you have done. But it does mean that you are not hopeless. Recognizing that a positive, God-given intention or need underlies your offensive actions or traits gives you a productive place to begin changing your behavior. Think about it. If a positive intention or need is not behind the obnoxious, even sinful, things we do, then we are merely evil people who are incapable of developing noble traits and habits. We have no hope that we will change; we must merely accept that we are impossibly screwed up, throw ourselves on God's mercy, and hope for the best.

But this pessimistic view runs completely counter to the notion that Christ has redeemed us and that in him all things are made new. One of the privileges of being a new creation in Christ is being given eyes to see ourselves as God sees us. As children of God, we are empowered to see through our sin, our weaknesses, and our limitations and discover the power of Christ shining out from deep within us (see 2 Corinthians 12:7–10). For in our weakness, God's strength and goodness are revealed.

So how do we identify the positive intention or need behind our own offensive behaviors and sins? By making an honest assessment of the benefits we think we're getting as a result.

Chad was frustrated with himself because he often lost his patience at work. He was a steward in the mill, and his job required him to negotiate disputes between labor and management. Some days he didn't know who upset him more, his fellow union workers, with their constant demands over every petty thing, or management, whose policy seemed to be "Say no first. Think later." He found himself becoming more and more hostile toward people on the job, and he felt guilty about it. Unfortunately, the guilt left him with even fewer emotional resources with which to deal with the demands of the job effectively. When I asked him to think about how he benefited by losing his cool, he was confused at first. "Well, actually," he said, "it really isn't benefiting me at all. It's earning me a lot of enemies real quick."

I explained that this was the ultimate consequence of his actions, but I wanted him to consider the immediate consequences. When he became angry, how did the people he was dealing with respond differently from how they did when he remained calm? Chad responded that, at least at first, people seemed to take him more seriously when he lost his temper. When he didn't lose his cool, people weren't as quick to respond to his grievances. I suggested that perhaps the intention behind his "tantrums," as he called them, was to motivate the people around him. This was not the most respectful way to motivate others, and it was wearing him out as well, but it was one way to get the job done. He agreed with my analysis, and the rest of our sessions concentrated on other ways that he could respectfully and efficiently move the grievance process along.

After we identified the intention behind Chad's anger, he experienced a kind of peace about the whole thing. As he put it, "I used to get real down on myself because I felt out of control. But now that I understand what I was trying to do, I can just think about ways to do it better. I don't have to get so irritated with myself, because I know what to do to fix the problem—or at least how to try."

Brainstorm more respectful and efficient ways to meet that intention or need.

Once you discover the intention behind a problem behavior or undesirable personality trait, you can begin to brainstorm more respectful and efficient ways to meet that need.

Jonathan was a terrible procrastinator. He lived by the motto Never do today what you can put off until tomorrow. Unfortunately, his tendency to make promises he didn't keep or to start projects he didn't finish was eroding the trust his wife placed in him. "I think she's had it with me. I came home the other day and told her that I was going to paint the porch over the weekend, and she blew up. She told me that I could do whatever I wanted, but she'd believe it when she saw it. I asked her why she was so angry—she's usually so patient—and she said that I always promise to do things and then they don't get done, and she's tired of not being able to count on me."

Jonathan felt angry at himself for letting things get so out of control, and he felt resentful of his wife, although he wasn't sure why. Setting this last point aside, I asked him what he thought was the intention of his procrastination. At first he said he didn't know, but when I asked him what was the immediate consequence of his behavior, he said, "I guess the immediate benefit I get from saying, 'I'll do it tomorrow' is that I get to take some time off. I'm usually pretty tired at the end of the day, and I don't want to disappoint my wife by saying I won't do such and such, but I just don't have it in me at that point."

As we talked, we realized that he resented his wife because he felt that she wasn't respecting his (unstated) need for downtime. "But," he said, "that's kind of stupid. I mean, how can she know that I need downtime if I don't tell her? I suppose she could guess by me sitting around like a log all night, but she could just as easily guess that I don't care about her." This, of course, was exactly what she was guessing.

I suggested that a more respectful and efficient way to meet his need would be to use the "Never negotiate the what; always negotiate the how and when" rule. To use this rule in his situation, Jonathan needed to acknowledge the things that had to be done around the house while openly stating his need to get some rest. He and his wife didn't need to argue about whose need would get met tonight; they needed to determine how and when they could meet both their needs.

During the following week, much progress was made. Before he left work to come home, Jonathan made it a point to call his wife to find out what was on her agenda for the evening as well as to let her know what he needed to do to let off some steam. "Most nights," he explained, "we decided to work on a project—whatever it was—until about 7:30, instead of the all-night marathons we used to do. This way, she knows that I am making an effort to get things done, and I know that after 7:30 I can either take some time for myself or play with the kids."

Rather than give in to his procrastinating tendencies, Jonathan was able to be honest about his needs with his wife and arrive at some ways they could work together to meet both of their needs. Using this approach—identifying the positive intention behind the behavior and brainstorming more respectful and efficient alternatives to express it—allowed Jonathan and his wife to rout out the passive-aggressiveness and resentment that were taking a toll on their marriage and replace them with a spirit of cooperation, understanding, and intimacy.

While Jonathan's problem is fairly innocent and common, the same strategy he used can help you overcome more serious personal struggles with problems like depression and anxiety disorders.

Andee called me at the Institute to see if I could help her overcome her struggle with anxiety. "I just feel so stressed all the time. Lately, I started getting this tightness in my chest when I think about all the things I have to do. My doctor tells me there's nothing physically wrong. It's just stress. That's why I called. I knew when the stress started making me sick that I had better do something about it. I just don't know what. I mean, the obvious answer is to cut back on my obligations, but I don't know how I can. I can't stand to let people down, but I can't keep going like this. I'm angry with myself because this nervousness makes me feel weak, and I HATE that. What can I do?"

As Andee talked, it became clear to me that a positive intention was behind the anxiety she felt. Many people who experience anxiety struggle with two things: the inability to say no to people and the need to feel that others approve of them. People who experience anxiety may need to take a break or seek the help of others, but since they can't do this on their own, they let their anxiety do the talking for them. Anxiety

- gives the person an excuse to say no: "I just feel too sick/overwhelmed to do any more."
- invites others to step in and offer help that the anxious person feels too guilty to ask for: "You look so stressed. Stop working yourself so hard; let me help!"
- lets the person gain approval for his or her harried efforts: "I don't know how you do it! You really handle a lot of things."

When I suggested these ideas, Andee was resistant at first. "I'm not trying to do that on purpose," she told me. I said that I understood that she wasn't consciously intending to do any of those things, but I wanted her to consider the immediate consequences of her anxiety. When she thought about it this way, she came to a startling conclusion. "You know, now that you mention it, when I get really stressed, my husband steps in and insists that I take a break. He even helps out more around the house. Usually he's more of a hang-out-and-watch-the-tube kind of guy when he's at home. And I usually don't ask for help. I figure if someone wants to help me, they'll offer. After all, that's what I do."

I assured her that her anxiety was real, that it wasn't as if she was intentionally making herself anxious in an attempt to get her husband to be more attentive and involved. Rather, her subconscious mind, working overtime while she was distracted with the busyness of everyday life, very cleverly came up with a solution to a problem she felt too guilty to solve on her own. Once she understood the intentions behind her anxiety—the need to get a break and ask for help—we spent several sessions coming up with more respectful and efficient ways she could meet those needs. For example, she needed to learn when it was acceptable to help others and when she needed to say no. She needed to recognize when she was approaching her limit and be comfortable asking for help. And finally, she needed to have a talk with her husband about what he could do around the house without waiting to be asked. These things did not come naturally to Andee, but when she practiced them, she became much calmer. Why? Because the intention behind her anxiety was being met in a more respectful, efficient manner.

Whether the problem that plagues your life is a simple one or more complex, a positive need or intention is always attempting to be expressed. If you can find it and can brainstorm more respectful and efficient alternatives for meeting those needs, you are well on your way to forgiving yourself and effecting positive change in your life.

Develop a plan for using those more respectful and efficient methods.

It is a regular occurrence. I will be counseling someone, and we will identify certain things that need to change in his or her life. Then I ask, "What do you think you'll need to do to make those things happen?"

Often the answer is some version of "I don't know. I guess I just have to make up my mind to do it." Unfortunately, this rarely works. Simply knowing what you need to do differently isn't often enough to get you to actually do it. That's why it's absolutely essential to develop a specific plan for changing your behavior.

Barb felt overwhelmed by work and household responsibilities. Her way of dealing with this was to be in a constant state of tension, worrying about home when she was at work and worrying about work when she was home. We identified that the intention behind her worry was "to help me remember everything that needs to be done." We even brainstormed a new way to meet that intention. Every day, Barb was to make a short list of the things that needed to be done, number them according to priority, and concentrate on accomplishing the top five things on her list every day. She told me that if she could do that, she would feel comfortable letting the other things go for a day, and she could relax a bit, knowing that she had a real plan for getting to everything. When I asked her what she needed to do to be able to implement her plan, she said, "Nothing. I think I can just decide to do it." I took her at her word.

Unfortunately, by the next week, nothing had changed. "I know, I know," she said. "I was supposed to make that list. I just kept forgetting. I would get out the door and think, 'Aaaa! I didn't do the list thing,' but by then it was too late and I would spend the whole day trying to keep everything in my head—and not being able to concentrate on anything."

I asked her again what she could do to help herself remember to implement her plan. At first, she didn't know, but as she thought more about it, she decided that if she put a note on her bathroom mirror and set the clock to wake her up fifteen minutes earlier, she would be more likely to remember and have the time to make her list.

A week later, she had made a dramatic improvement. Three out of five workdays, Barb was able to use her list, and it made such a difference in both her tension level and her organizational abilities that she vowed to do it every day from then on.

As you can see from Barb's experience, sometimes even the best intentions in the world cannot help us make the changes we need to make. We have to develop a specific plan to support the changes we want to make or we will continue to be frustrated. This is especially true with more serious problems.

Derrick was a workaholic who thrived on the pressures and challenges at work. Unfortunately, as admirable as his work ethic was, it caused him to be fairly neglectful of his family. For years, his wife and children coped adequately with Derrick's absences, but lately his oldest son, Peter, had been getting in trouble at school and had been more noncompliant at home. In family counseling, Peter revealed that one of the biggest reasons he had been acting up was to show his dad how angry he was for his dad not being around.

It was obvious even to Derrick that he needed to find a way to spend more time with his family. But how? We brainstormed several options and finally settled on a plan.

Derrick decided that at least once a month he would take each of his children out for some one-on-one time. Likewise, every week the family was to schedule some kind of activity that they would engage in together. Derrick would sit down with his wife at the beginning of each month and write down these "family appointments" in his calendar, keeping them as he would any other business meeting.

Everyone seemed satisfied with the plan. Nevertheless, it was more difficult to follow than anyone had expected. The first month they tried it, Derrick and his wife neglected to have their planning meeting before the first of the month. Because Derrick's schedule fills up so quickly, by the time they got around to planning the family time, most of his calendar was full. Derrick was able to make time to take Peter out that month, but he continued to be absent from the other children's lives and was not a part of any other family activities.

It would have been easy for Derrick or the family to become frustrated at this point. One could easily have said that if the family were really important to Derrick, he would have made time for them. But at this point in the game, such a tactic would have simply undermined the process. In light of Derrick's efforts to at least make time for Peter, I decided to give him the benefit of the doubt. Instead of criticizing him (or allowing him to wallow in his own feelings of guilt and frustration), I asked him what it would take to do better next month.

Derrick sighed, and after giving it a few moments of thought, he sheepishly said, "I know this sounds pathetic, but if Jacqueline [his wife] and I don't actually schedule our monthly planning time, it's just never going to happen." I thanked him for his suggestion and asked if he had his book with him. He did. During that session, Derrick and his wife scheduled monthly meetings—in his book—for the remainder of the year. When they got home, she was to put them on the family calendar.

At the end of the session, I asked to speak to Derrick alone for a minute. I first reinforced Derrick's intention to follow through by thanking him for sticking with his family on this instead of getting defensive. But I also stressed that having made the promise to have these family meetings and having scheduled them out, he needed to follow through with them if he wanted to see his next anniversary. (His wife had been on the brink of calling an attorney before they began counseling. The sessions had bought them some time, but change needed to happen soon.) He had too little emotional stock with the family to ask them to extend to him any more credit. He said that he understood, and he reasserted his desire to reconnect with his family.

As the year progressed, Derrick and his family did make significant progress. The monthly meetings happened as scheduled, and the family times were faithfully kept. The family still missed him and he continued to struggle with balancing work and family. But because Derrick was making it a point to be there much more often than he had been in the past, the tension was decreasing in the family, Peter's behavior was improving, and even Jacqueline felt closer to Derrick. All along, Derrick had the best of intentions, but he needed a specific plan to help him stay faithful to those intentions.

Too many times, people become frustrated with themselves if at first they don't succeed. What is needed in these times is not self-flagellation, but a better plan. When you get stuck despite your best intentions and your clearly stated goals, ask yourself what kind of additional support you need to achieve those goals, and then go get it. Chances are you will be better off than if you just sit around navel gazing, asking, "What's wrong with me?" over and over until you decide you are a hopeless case. Just remember: God believes in you. Otherwise he wouldn't have made you. You are not a hopeless case. You merely struggle, like the rest of us. Welcome to humanity, my friend. Pick up your cross, follow him, and you just might get to rise from your own humiliation as well.

Evaluate the plan and make improvements.

Change is like pants. (Hear me out now.) After a while, you grow out of it and you need to try on something new. Just because you had a plan that worked for you six months ago doesn't mean that you have to stick with it for the rest of your life. Even though Derrick's involvement with his family had vastly increased, a year from now, when the monthly dates with his children and the weekly family times have become second nature, Derrick will need to revisit his plan and see if there isn't more he can be doing.

It happens with some regularity that I get a call from a client who I saw several years before and who feels the need to reconnect because she is having to deal with a new manifestation of an old problem. Often, this client feels frustrated with herself and will make the comment "I thought I had this beat. Why now?"

As therapy progresses, the answer to a client's "Why now?" almost inevitably becomes apparent. Usually, it has something to do with the person entering a new stage of life; the old strategies simply are not as relevant as they once were. One woman who had recovered from depression experienced another episode several years later when her youngest son went off to college. She was very disappointed in herself, and in our first meeting she expressed a great deal of self-criticism for her "weakness" and "backsliding." After she finished venting, I reminded her that the last time I had seen her, the core of her depression was her feeling that the work she was doing (being a homemaker) was not as important or as interesting as some of her friends' careers. At the time, she was comparing herself to them and, in her estimation, coming up short. She chuckled when she remembered this, saying that she hadn't thought of that in years.

Furthermore, I continued, the last time she had been in counseling, her "cure" had been to rediscover the worth of what she was doing. We had discussed the possibility of her pursuing a career for a while, but over time, and as she reconnected with the reasons she had originally quit her law practice to concentrate on full-time mothering, she had nixed the idea. As I saw it, the problem was not that she was backsliding but that the old strategy of coping with the depression (reconnecting with the importance of her motherhood, being—as she put it—"a professional mom") had become obsolete when her son had left home. What she was experiencing was the call to move on to a new stage in life, to discover a new contribution she could make to society. I suspected that once she decided that she was not, in fact, obsolete, she would be just fine.

She seemed pleased and surprised by what I suggested. Over the next few weeks, we talked about the contribution she might like to make to her family and to society now that her children needed her in a different, less hands-on way. The one thing she kept coming back to was writing. She had always enjoyed writing, and she had won a few contests and had published a couple of articles over the years. I suggested that she dust off her word-processing skills and see what happened.

The change was remarkable. As she told me in our next session, "I went back and read some of my older stuff, and—this is kind of embarrassing—it was pretty good. I started thinking that maybe I could do this. At the very least, it can't hurt to try. I sent some query letters to a couple of magazines, and, well, we'll see what happens."

I asked about her mood, and she told me, "I think you were right. Being valuable and making a contribution has always been important to me. If I feel like I'm getting ready to be put in mothballs, it makes me nuts. I should have remembered from the last time [I was in therapy] that the intention behind my depressive episodes is to help me rediscover my sense of purpose. I just felt so lost. But now that I think I've found a direction, I've been a lot better this past week. I'm hopeful, anyway."

I saw her for another month before she told me that she felt confident enough to go it alone again, but the fact was that nothing was really wrong with her. She had merely outgrown the last change she'd made, and it was time for a new plan.

When you find old habits coming back or, conversely, when you have attained a certain level of mastery over those habits, ask yourself if you haven't outgrown the changes you made and if it isn't time to either come up with a new plan or improve upon the old one.

Until the day we die, we will be works in progress. The bad news is that we're never done growing, changing, revisiting old ghosts, reconquering lost ground, and achieving new goals. But the good news is that we're never done growing, changing, revisiting old ghosts, reconquering lost ground, and achieving new goals. As long as we remember that God dwells within us, there will always be hope for us. Likewise, as long as we remind ourselves of the God-given intentions or needs that underlie our problem behaviors, take the time to consider them, and constantly look for more respectful ways to express them, there will always be hope for us. We will remain loveable, as C. S. Lewis once wrote, not so much on our own merits, but because "love Himself" dwells within us.

Love Your Neighbor as Yourself

Of course, the downside to learning how to love yourself is that all of a sudden it isn't as much fun to pick on other people anymore. The logic goes like this: If a positive intention or need is behind the stupid things *I* do, and if I want others to recognize that and not pick on me anymore, how can I possibly apply anything but a similar generous spirit toward others?

Of course, there will be times when we slip. Our baser instincts will occasionally cause us to write someone off or enjoy a bit of schadenfreude. Yet once we truly realize how we—yes, even we—are loveable in the eyes of God, it will never be as much fun to stay in those self-righteous places as it used to be.

We all know—at least on an intellectual level—that God loves us. And so, on an intellectual level, we can grudgingly love other people. But once we cross the bridge to understanding the mechanics of how God is able to love us (that is, by being able to see through all the dreck and witness the good intention or need struggling to get out), instead of merely taking it on faith, then we can no longer help but extend a similar courtesy to others.

As I wrote in chapter 1, when I first came to this realization, it was a very liberating experience. I had always known that God loved me, but I now had a sense of how that was possible, and I was in awe of God's ability to love me in this way. It made me want to treat others the same way. Heaven knows, I'm still far from perfect at it, but what a wonderful thing it is to be able to get a glimpse of myself as God sees me and then be able, more often then not, to see others in the same light. The better I get at it, the less angry and judgmental I become. Likewise, the better I get at applying these techniques to myself, the less susceptible I am to irrational guilt and self-criticism.

I invite you to discover this joy for yourself. Allow yourself to see not just that God loves you but how that is possible, and you will begin to see a change in your attitude toward others. You will finally be able to understand, on a truly experiential level, what Jesus meant when he said, "Love your neighbor as you love yourself."

Changing Your World: How to Keep Getting Better

Blessed are the peacemakers.

~ MATTHEW 5:9

Now that you're armed with a healthy sense of your own basic goodness and desirability in the eyes of God, it's time to spread a little of that love around. In this chapter, we'll focus on what it takes to create change in your marriage, with your children, and in the world at large.

Some of what we will discuss in this chapter we have discussed in earlier chapters, but this time we will look at specific strategies for each type of relationship. Some of the approaches you use to bring about change in your marriage will be less effective or appropriate when used to handle problems in the workplace. Likewise, you will need to set different limits with your friends or your boss from those you set with your spouse or children. This may seem very obvious on the face of it, but when it comes to applying these techniques it sometimes gets a little more complicated.

One metaphor I like to use in counseling sessions is that of the carpenter's apprentice who was very good with a hammer. In fact, he loved using the hammer so much that he tried to use it for every job. Besides using it to pound nails, he tried to use it to saw wood, install windows, paint, and so on. As we might expect, he met with decidedly mixed results. The point is that many of us, having discovered a tool that works well for us, try to use that same tool in all of our relationships, becoming frustrated when it works with one person but not with another.

The husband in one couple I used to counsel was a physician on an emergency helicopter medical team. His work required him to make quick, brutal decisions about what needed to be done and who needed to do it. He always made sure he knew what he was talking about before he spoke (and if he didn't, he was good at deferring to colleagues more experienced than himself), but once he spoke, he expected to be obeyed immediately. He was a very efficient, take-charge person and, generally speaking, a very likeable fellow. The problem was that he not only used this kind of take-charge style at work, where it was appropriate, but he also used it with his family, where it was both less appropriate and less effective. His wife would complain of his "bullying" manner, and he would complain of her "stubbornness." Complicating things was the fact that, technically speaking, he was usually right. The problem was that he tended to use an "I have spoken!" communication style that caused his family to resent and fear him. Only after he learned that he could not use the same communication style in every context was he finally able to communicate his intentions effectively. By using a different, more collegial approach, this man was able to show his family the love and care he was trying to express to them and the logic behind the opinions he held.

Love Your (Closest) Neighbor

Jesus tells us that we are to love our neighbor. We will examine our response to this command beginning with our closest neighbors, our spouse and children, and then we'll work out from there.

Love your spouse.

It takes a lot to have a successful marital relationship, and I cover this topic much more broadly in another book, *For Better...Forever!* But if I had to boil everything in that book down to three tips for having a solid marital relationship, I would offer these three rules.

- Follow the 5:1 rule religiously.
- Always, always, always assume a positive intention.
- Live the "Never negotiate the what; always negotiate the how and when" rule.

Let's briefly examine each of these as they apply to marriage.

Follow the 5:1 rule religiously. In order for a husband and wife to be able to deal gracefully with the problems of life and marriage, it is essential that they follow the 5:1 rule. This rule states that you must be at least five times more complimentary, supportive, encouraging, affectionate, and generous than you are complaining, critical, argumentative, or demanding.

While following this rule is necessary for any relationship to run smoothly, maintaining the 5:1 ratio is absolutely critical for a solid marriage. The amount of defensiveness, circular arguing (repetitive arguments that don't go anywhere), and resentment a couple experiences in problem solving is a direct indicator of how well (or how poorly) they are living the 5:1 rule. When a couple enjoys five times more positivity than negativity in its interactions, defensiveness and arguing decrease dramatically. Likewise, when the ratio is off, spouses are quickly at each other's throats.

The best way I know for a couple to make certain that they are maintaining a 5:1 ratio is for them to make a "love list." To do this, both the husband and the wife must write down (on separate sheets of paper) as many things as they can think of that make them feel loved or cared for. Most of these should be simple things. For instance, "I love when you look at me when I talk to you instead of staring at the computer" or "I like when you sit on the same piece of furniture with me and hold me while we watch TV instead of going across the room."

I encourage couples to write down as many things as they can think of so that each person will have many options to choose from. Next, the husband and the wife exchange their lists, make a few copies, and post them in conspicuous places (the mirror, the refrigerator, the car dashboard) so that they can't forget them. Finally, each day the husband and the wife make themselves responsible for doing as many things on the lists as possible, regardless of their mood that day. The point of the exercise is to remind the husband and wife that they have a responsibility to be as loving to each other as possible. Further, it reminds both the husband and the wife to make their marriage a priority, and it offers practical ways to maintain the 5:1 rule.

My favorite story of how this technique works comes from a couple I counseled by phone at the Institute. They had been fighting terribly for two weeks prior to the session, and there was no end in sight. In the course of our meeting, I explained that they would have to rebuild rapport before they would be able to solve any of their problems, and then I outlined how they could use these "love lists" to help them regain that rapport. Initially, they were resistant. They wanted to fight, not love. But as they explained in their next session, a funny thing happened.

"When we first got off the phone, we started fighting right away," said Chip, the husband. "I was still really steamed, and I just couldn't stop. But after a few minutes, I just saw how completely useless it was to go on like this. I mean, we'd beaten this to death for two weeks and hadn't gotten anywhere. I just looked at Melanie and said—more in frustration than anything else—'Why don't we both just shut up and do what Greg says?' " (I have since decided to print this slogan on all of my business cards—just kidding.)

They agreed to at least try what I had suggested, and so for the next week they called a moratorium on discussing their problems and just concentrated on building rapport. They made a point to be polite to each other even though it seemed forced at first, and they did the love-lists exercise, making sure to do a few thoughtful things for each other every day—"even though neither one of us felt like doing anything for the other," Melanie later confided. As the week went on, things warmed up considerably. Both Chip and Melanie knew their problems hadn't gone away, but they appreciated the sincere effort each was making to reclaim their friendship and look out for each other again. A week later, at their next appointment, we were able to resolve two of their most difficult issues quickly and with little resistance from either person.

As Chip explained, "It was really hard to do what you said at first, but as the week went by, it was like God was pouring out a lot of grace on both of us, and we realized how selfish we were both being. We were acting like we both wanted our own way no matter what. That's not what marriage is about. I know I was ashamed of how I'd been acting. I do love her, after all. Even though she drives me nuts sometimes. [They both chuckled.] Then, when we started taking better care of each other throughout the week, it just made sense to keep it up when we got back to talking about our problems in the session."

If you and your spouse are experiencing a stalemate, the first thing to do is take a break from the discussion (with the understanding that you will come back to it later) and work on the friendship. After you have reconfirmed your mutual commitment to look out for each other's best interests, resume the discussion with fresh perspective. This is the married couple's way of living out the biblical injunction to "leave your gift at the altar" and make peace with your neighbor.

Always, always, always assume a positive intention. We have talked about this at length throughout the book, but in no relationship is this injunction more important—and more difficult to enact—than in marriage.

Many people think that their spouse wakes up with a "twenty-five ways to tick off my husband/wife" list in mind, and they treat each other accordingly. This is simply not true. First, your husband or wife loves you and would never do anything to intentionally harm you. (*The only time you cannot use this rule is in cases of abuse or addiction. Granted, a positive intention is behind even these behaviors, but it is beyond your ability to cope with them. In these situations, professional help is needed.*) Second, even if you doubted your spouse's love for you, he would still not intentionally harm you, because you know where he sleeps! He is not stupid. He knows that any stupid thing he does can and will be used against him. Finally, even if your partner does "intend" to be hurtful (for example, he yells at you or talks down to you), it is probably because he has tried and has failed to communicate his message in several other, more respectful ways.

One of the ideas I try to impress upon all the couples I counsel is that any time a person thinks his or her partner is out to get them, they are thinking irrationally. Yes, that's right. You are thinking irrationally, and before you say another word, you have to get your own head screwed on straight.

The best way to do this is to become a master at those clarifying questions we discussed earlier. Remember, when you ask a clarifying question you say, "When you did (describe the situation, but don't analyze), it seemed like (explain how her action came across), *but what did you really mean by that*?" This last part of the question is the most important because it shows that you assume a positive intention is behind the offensive behavior. Keep asking the "What did you mean by that?" question until you get an answer that actually sounds like a positive intention.

For example, imagine a wife walks through the door and finds her husband sitting in his recliner. Suddenly she screams.

Wife: You are such a jerk sometimes!

Husband (stung, but he just read this great book so he's going to try something new): Well, what do you mean by that?

Wife: I mean you never think of anyone but yourself!

Husband (thinking, *This isn't going very well, but Greg said to keep trying until I understand the intention*): Well, what do mean by *that*?

Wife: I *mean* that you completely forgot that my car was in the shop and that you had to pick me up from work today. I had to hitchhike home with a group of Hare Krishnas.

Husband (who now realizes the positive intention behind his wife's "attack"): Uh-oh...

Silliness aside, you get the point. Whenever you think that your spouse is out to get you, chances are you are not thinking rationally. Ask clarifying questions to discover the positive intention behind an offensive action and then work with him or her to resolve the problem.

Live the "Never negotiate the what; always negotiate the how and when" rule. You are not your spouse's parent. You may not, under any circumstances, act as if it is your place to grant or deny permission for anything your spouse wants to do.

When I say this, the first reaction most people have is "Well, what if she wants to do some boneheaded thing!" My response to this is "You were supposed to rule out the boneheads before you got married. Now, having married one (or so you say), you are obliged to work with her to help her find respectful ways to get what she wants."

That said, the only time this rule does not apply is when your spouse is dealing with addictions or other serious (and diagnosable) mental/emotional problems that prevent him or her from functioning in a normal, healthy manner.

At the same time, refusing to deny your partner any objectively reasonable thing she asks for does not require you to automatically give in to everything she wants, the way she wants it, when she wants it. You have every right to express your concerns and insist that before your partner does something, she work with you to find a mutually respectful way to meet that need.

Most married couples' fights (as opposed to mere arguments) result from the husband and wife feeling as if each one's needs are not being respected by the other. Carl wanted Lindsay to be more passionate in their marriage. Lindsay, however, had grown up in a home where emotional displays were frowned upon, affection was rarely shared, and sexuality was rarely discussed unless it was being condemned in some form. Needless to say, there was a great deal of tension in their marriage. What made matters worse, though, was that rather than Lindsay saying to Carl, "I have a hard time being as physically intimate as you want me to be, but if you'll be patient with me and help me, I am willing to grow," she tended to say, "I have a hard time being physically affectionate, but you knew that when we got married so you'll just have to get over it." It is one thing to admit to your partner that you have concerns about his needs or have areas of weakness that require patience and understanding on his part. It is another thing to tell your partner that you think what he wants is stupid.

When our husband or wife asks for something, we have a right to express our concerns, to ask for help, to insist upon finding a way to meet the stated need in a manner and time frame that are respectful to our own values, priorities, and goals. However, assuming that our partner's request does not endanger our physical health or our moral well-being, we may never, ever suggest that something he or she wants is stupid, crazy, or beneath us.

Never negotiate what your spouse is asking you for. But always feel free to negotiate the manner and the time frame in which you meet that need.

While all of the techniques outlined in *God Help Me! These People Are Driving Me Nuts* can be useful to you in your marriage, the three we just covered are the ones you will want to focus on in order to keep your marital relationship running smoothly. For other tips, check out the problem-solving chapter in *For Better . . . Forever!* or call the Pastoral Solutions Institute at (740) 266-6461.

Next we will examine the techniques you will want to focus on in your relationship with your children—especially your grown, wayward children.

Love Your (Difficult) Children.

I cover many parenting dilemmas in *Parenting with Grace: Catholic Parent's Guide to Raising (almost) Perfect Kids,* which I coauthored with my wife, Lisa. But while *God Help Me! These People Are Driving Me Nuts* is not a parenting book, sometimes the most difficult people to deal with are your children, especially your adult children who are making life choices that make you cringe.

I regularly get calls at the Pastoral Solutions Institute from parents whose adult children are leading faithless, self-destructive, or irresponsible lives. The calls follow a familiar pattern. "I did my best when they were growing up. I tried to give them everything I could, but now look how they're throwing their life/faith/marriage away. What can I do?"

Sometimes parents go on to lament that their child has now turned on them as well. "All I tried to do was to offer some advice. Now she won't even talk to me."

Marcia, the twenty-seven-year-old daughter of Jeane and Ralph, had a drinking problem. Actually, she had many problems, but the drinking especially had been getting out of hand lately. She no longer lived at home and regularly spurned her parents' offers to help, saying, "I don't have a problem and I really don't need your advice." Unfortunately, her life spoke volumes about the help she needed. This single mother of two seemed unable to keep a job and had recently been reported to children's services for neglecting her children while she was out at the local bar at night. Jeane and Ralph had stepped up to be the guardians of Marcia's children, but Marcia continued to live a self-destructive and irresponsible life, even to the point of skipping her visitation time with her children. Jeane and Ralph were heartbroken. On the one hand, they felt responsible (Ralph, though sober now for twenty years, had been a heavy drinker during the first ten years of Marcia's life). On the other hand, there was little they could do, because there was little that Marcia wanted them to do. They called the Institute to see if there was any way they could find some peace for themselves and, if Marcia would let them, discover some ways that they might be able to help her.

Bruce called the Institute because he wanted to know if it was possible to heal his relationship with his son, Perry. Perry was cohabiting with a woman who had left her husband and six-year-old daughter to move in with Perry. Bruce and Perry had always had a conflicted relationship, but the situation deteriorated once Perry became involved with Serena. Bruce was a very devout Catholic who struggled with how to remain true to church teaching while having a relationship with his son. Perry, for his part, rejected Bruce for "trying to run my life" and the Catholic Church for, as he put it, "its backward ideas about sex and its stupid rules about everything." But things went from bad to worse one Thanksgiving when Perry told his parents that either he would be permitted to bring Serena to the family dinner—and be allowed to stay in the same room with her in Bruce's home—or he would not come. Bruce didn't know what to do. He was angry. He was hurt and confused. "Perry knows how I feel about all this," Bruce told me. "Why would he want to rub my face in it?" Bruce did not wish to let his son think that he supported him in any way. And yet, said Bruce, "He's my son. I don't want to lose him completely."

When dealing with your adult children, it is important to keep four things in mind.

- You are not responsible for their choices.
- You have the right to set whatever limits you believe are necessary to maintaining your own physical, mental, moral, or financial health.
- You shouldn't offer to bring the potato salad before you're invited to the party. (Listen, but don't give unsolicited advice or help.)
- You should do whatever is reasonable to maintain the relationship.

Let's take a look at each of these points.

You are not responsible for their choices. When your children are young, you are obligated to do everything you can to provide for their physical, emotional, moral, and educational needs. If you were less than generous in any of these areas and this is an issue between you and your child, then you need to accept responsibility for your own errors and humbly ask your child's forgiveness. That said, even if you were the worst parent in the world—and I sincerely doubt that you were—the choices your children make in adulthood are their choices, not yours. Let me repeat, you are not responsible for your adult children's choices, even if they insist that it was you who "screwed them up" in the first place. It is one thing to accept responsibility for and repent of your own past mistakes. It is another thing to let them off the hook for getting themselves "un–screwed up."

Keeping this in mind can be very freeing for the parent, and it can also be freeing for the parent-child relationship. Too many times, parents of adult children feel that it is their obligation to make their children live a healthier, more moral, or more responsible life. They feel guilty for having done something wrong when raising their children, and so they try to make up for their earlier failure by lecturing and arguing with their children or, alternatively, by coddling them. Both kinds of interventions are doomed to fail. Once your children reach adulthood, it is not your job to make them do anything. It is not your job to fix them.

At the same time, it is your job to live your own life as a quiet witness to your children and to make whatever changes you need to make in your own life so that such a witness will be possible. It is your job to be as loving to your children as possible, as opposed to being openly critical, disgusted, or hostile. And it is your job to set limits with your children whenever necessary, such as when they treat you in a contemptuous manner or ask you to do things that endanger your own physical, mental, moral, or financial well-being. Beyond this, you need to back off. Once your children are adults, you need to give them to God in prayer and then get out of God's way. Their healing may take time; you may not live to see it. But Scripture promises that if you have faith the size of a mustard seed you can move mountains. Surely, that same faith in the saving power of Christ can accomplish your children's healing if you just let God take the wheel for you.

Now, even though you are not responsible for your children's choices, you are responsible for your reaction to those choices. This brings us to the second point.

You have the right to set whatever limits you believe are necessary to maintaining your own physical, mental, moral, or financial health. While charity requires us to be as generous to our children as we can be, sometimes our children will ask us for things that we simply cannot or should not give them. When your wayward adult child asks you for something, ask yourself the following questions.

- Can I respond to the request without *seriously* endangering my own physical, mental, moral, or financial well-being?
- Is he asking me to solve his problems? Or is he working hard, but just needs a little boost?

- Will fulfilling the request require me to commit a sin myself?

These are highly personal questions that only you can answer. Pray over these questions when trying to decide what you can and cannot do to help your struggling adult child. Ask God to give you the grace and wisdom you need to know the difference between the "time to act and the time to yield."

You shouldn't offer to bring the potato salad before you're invited to the party. When your child comes to you with a problem, the most important thing to do is listen. Avoid the temptation to lecture or even to give unsolicited advice. Most of the time your adult children really don't need your advice (even if you think they do). What they need is a sympathetic ear and room to figure out things for themselves. Feel free to ask if you can do anything (and be ready to fill any reasonable request), but avoid the temptation to solve the problem for your child. That is merely crippling.

That said, I want to make one clarification. Misfortune befalls everyone. If your child is struggling because of some event that is completely beyond his or her control, then Christian charity obliges you to generously volunteer any help you can give. On the other hand, if your child is experiencing misfortune due to his or her own irresponsibility or immorality, it is best to remain sympathetic but basically silent until he or she has come up with a plan for climbing out of the hole. Then, and only then, should you be willing to fulfill any reasonable requests for help. To put it another way, if your child falls into a hole, it is fine to provide her with the wood to build a ladder as long as she builds it herself and climbs out of the hole of her own free will. It is quite another thing for your child to fall into a hole and then expect you to provide the wood, build the ladder, and drag her kicking and screaming out of the hole.

You should do whatever is reasonable to maintain the relationship. Sometimes our children ask us to do things that make us uncomfortable but really pose no danger to our physical, moral, mental, or financial health. When that is the case, Christian charity obliges us to overcome our own pettiness and make the necessary effort to help them.

Bruce and Perry's Thanksgiving Day dilemma is a fairly good example of this principle at work. At first, Bruce felt he had to refuse Perry's request to bring Serena to Bruce's home, much less allow them to room together, because Bruce did not wish to imply in any way that he supported their relationship. In effect, Bruce was concerned that he was putting his own moral well-being in jeopardy if he did not stand in rigid opposition to his son's relationship with Serena. But as Bruce considered the situation further, he felt that he needed to make a distinction between the moral stand he needed to make to be true to his beliefs and the rigid attitude he was projecting simply because he was angry with Perry. Obviously, Bruce could not allow Perry and Serena to room together in his home, but Bruce felt that he could allow Perry to bring Serena to dinner as long as they conducted themselves as mere friends during their visit. He decided to tell Perry that Serena would be welcome for dinner, but they could not room together in his house. Bruce and his wife, Ann, would give Serena a separate room in their home, or Perry could make other arrangements, but Perry and Serena would be welcome to the home and to dinner if they could abide by these limits. Bruce and Ann decided to do this—even though it made them uncomfortable—for two reasons. First, Bruce and Ann felt that they would have more opportunities to influence their son if they did not completely alienate him. Second, Bruce and Ann hoped that perhaps, in some small way, their own relationship could be a witness to Perry and Serena. Bruce and Ann had not always been as happy together as they were now. In fact, they suspected that their conflicted marriage when Perry was young had a great deal to do with Perry's less-than-stellar relationship history. Ann especially hoped that at some point over the visit, she and Bruce could share their own story with Serena in the hopes of subtly encouraging her to return to her husband and daughter. Likewise, they hoped that the weekend would give Perry—who had not spent any extended time with his parents for several years—the opportunity to see how much Bruce and Ann's relationship had healed over the years.

Bruce told a surprised Perry that Serena would be welcome to come to Thanksgiving dinner. However, Bruce also explained his conditions. Bruce told Perry that he sincerely hoped that Perry and Serena would come. He even apologized for his harsh attitude in the past. But he hoped Perry would understand that he could not offend his own beliefs by allowing Perry and Serena to room together. As far as Bruce and Ann were concerned, Serena was a close friend to Perry, and she would be welcomed as such. At first

Perry balked, but he eventually decided to accept his parents' charitable and prudent compromise and brought Serena to dinner only. The situation remained somewhat awkward, but as Bruce put it, "It was the closest I have felt to my son in five years. I was able to stay faithful to my beliefs and still let him know that there is always a place in my heart for him. I think it was at least a good start."

By doing whatever is reasonable to salvage the relationship you have with your children while setting healthy limits, you increase the chances that they will think of you as a reasonable person, and therefore you increase the chances that one day they will be willing to accept what you have to say about their life and choices.

Of course, the most important thing you can ever do for your errant adult children is pray for their well-being and their growth in a life of faith and clear moral vision. But just as faith without work is dead, so too is prayer without service. You must do what you can to be a loving model of Christ to your children, offering limits when necessary but always in a greater context of true Christian love and charity.

As our last step in discussing how to change your world and keep the change, I'd like to take a few moments to talk about the other people in your life—employers, friends, and others, who, although they are perhaps not as close to you as your spouse and children are, still manage to find a way to get under your skin.

Love Your (Other) Neighbor

Jeanette's supervisor, Marlee, was a difficult person. She tended to allow her personal feelings to dictate the way she treated those under her. If she liked you, you were "in," regardless of your actual job performance. If she didn't, as Jeanette colorfully put it, "you could show up for work gold plated and still be treated like sh**."

Jeanette explained that, generally speaking, she considered herself to be an effective person, but that in Marlee's presence she became a nervous wreck. "I hate the way she treats people, and I hate the way I feel around her, but I don't know what to do."

Marcy was Catelin's next-door neighbor. Catelin complained that she constantly felt judged by Marcy, who regularly criticized, among other things, the way Catelin raised her children and managed her household. Complicating matters was the fact that Marcy was in charge of many of the organizations in which Catelin was involved, so it wouldn't do to offend her, as Marcy would only end up making Catelin's life that much more difficult. Even so, it was getting to the point where something had to be done. As Catelin put it, "I feel terrible saying it. I mean, I know it's not the Christian thing to feel, but just looking at that woman makes my flesh crawl. I need to figure out how to make her back off—without shooting myself in the foot."

Whether at work or in the community, Christians are constantly challenged by relationships. How can you remain true to your beliefs while still functioning well at work? How can you maintain your priorities so that lesser relationships and involvements do not sap the energy you reserve for the more important areas of your life? Because every person's circumstances are unique, it would be difficult within the pages of this book to come up with solutions for every possible problem that could occur between you and all the people in your everyday life. Even so, I will offer two techniques, the ideal-self exercise and the priorities exercise, to help you find your own answers to the most difficult situations. These two exercises work by helping us maintain our focus and develop a specific, workable plan for handling conflict in all of the relationships in our lives.

THE IDEAL SELF: AN EXERCISE

This exercise is based on the Christian idea that everything that happens in the course of a day is an opportunity to grow in greater strength and virtue and can help us become the person God created us to be. The best way to teach the exercise is to lead you through it one step at a time.

Pick a problem. Pick a situation in which you feel that you are not responding in the best possible way. It could be anything, from trouble at the office to a conflict with the neighbors or even a problem with your spouse or children. Try to be as specific as possible about what bothers you. Avoid generalizations. For example, don't write, "John really bugs me." Instead, write, "I hate when John yells at me about the sales reports." Once you have a situation in mind, write it down.

Identify your current response. Next, think of how you currently respond to the situation at hand. To continue our example, you might write, "When John yells at me about the sales reports, I freeze up and don't say anything." Write down how you respond to your problem situation.

Identify the personal resources you need. Now ask yourself what qualities you would need to handle the situation more effectively. Would it be helpful if you were stronger in the situation? more compassionate? had a better sense of humor? felt more confident? If you aren't sure about what qualities it would be most helpful to have, think about the gifts and fruits of the Holy Spirit—wisdom, counsel, understanding, fortitude, knowledge, piety, reverence for God—or the virtues of faith, hope, love, prudence, justice, and temperance. Other qualities that are perhaps less spiritual but often just as helpful include wit, creativity, cheerfulness, caution, and emotional security. Which of these qualities might help you respond to the problem situation in a manner that would make you feel especially proud? Again, to return to our example of John yelling at you about the sales reports, you might write, "I need to have a better sense of humor about it and not take it so personally, but I also need to have the courage to tell him when he is going too far." Once you have identified certain qualities you believe would be helpful to you, write them down.

Envision your ideal response. Now, I want you to imagine your "ideal self." That is, the self God wants you to cooperate with his grace to become. Keep in mind that when I say "ideal self," I don't mean the you that walks on water or never gets angry. Rather, I mean the you that has all the normal internal feelings and struggles but is able to rise to the occasion *in spite of* feeling angry or frustrated or irritable. How would your ideal self use the qualities you just identified to respond to the problem situation? Be specific. Don't just write, "My ideal self would have a good sense of humor about this." Write what that would look like. "When John yells at me about the sales reports, I will salute him and cheerfully say, 'Sir, yes sir.' If he seems offended, I will just smile, pat him on the shoulder, and say, 'I promise they will be in on time. Hey, have I ever failed you before?' and then I'll go back to work."

Write down your ideal response.

Some people find it helpful to actually visualize themselves acting in the ideal way. Play the scene out in your head. Make corrections as needed. The point is not to change how the other person is responding but to make sure you are extremely proud of the way you are responding to the situation.

Once you have identified how you want your ideal self to respond, make yourself stick to your plan, and the next time the situation occurs, act as if you really are your ideal self. At first it will feel awkward, even forced, but go ahead and do it anyway. The point is that by putting your best foot forward—even if only for pretend—you will eventually become your ideal self in that situation. This is what C. S. Lewis called "playing dress-up," that is, the Christian practice of putting on virtues we have not yet mastered in the hopes of one day growing into them.

The Ideal Self

Some people have a hard time envisioning their ideal response. They say, "How do I know what will work?" Usually what that means is "What if my response doesn't change the other person?" This is missing the point entirely. You cannot change the other person. The best you can do is make sure that your response is consistent with the virtues and qualities you identified in the last exercise. If you are responding to a problem situation in a manner that you are proud of, you have succeeded, regardless of how crazy the other person is acting. Granted, your hope may be that the other person will be positively influenced by your example. Likewise, if he or she is not, you may eventually be forced to end the relationship. Even so, by responding to the problem as your ideal self would, you are doing all that you can do to solve your piece of the problem. The rest is up to the other person, and even if the situation is not resolved, you can go about your business with a clear conscience (for not having taken the bait) and with a deep sense of satisfaction (for having risen to the challenge and done your best).

We must constantly struggle against the temptation to believe that our own happiness is dependent upon our getting everyone else to behave just as we want them to behave. Real happiness comes from self-mastery, from having the ability to get *ourselves* to behave just as we ought to behave. Once we learn how to do that, other people's craziness will not bother us nearly as much, because even when other people are out of control, we will feel in control of ourselves.

Perhaps a personal example will help. While I do not wish to hold myself up as some sort of model, I do happen to be pretty good at keeping my cool when other people around me are losing theirs. There are many times in my practice when I encounter a couple who are screaming at each other so much that I am sure I will have to clean their blood off the walls before I go home that night. Similarly, there have been plenty of times when I have been attacked personally and professionally for many different reasons.

In these situations, my first temptation is to focus on the other person's behavior, to try to get him to see the error of his ways, to argue with him and change him. However, I find that when I do this, I begin to feel myself becoming as irrational as he seems to me. I feel angry, tense, and out of control, and the more I continue down this path, the more irrational, desperate, and ineffective I become. So, rather than waste my energy thinking, *What can I do to change him?* (a desperate and ineffective question), I concentrate all of my efforts on answering the following question: *What do I need to do to appear both respectful and firm in this situation?* By concentrating on the two qualities I most need to function at my best, I am able to see specifically how I need to respond to the problem. Even though I may be quaking with anger, fear, or frustration on the inside, because I am concentrating my energy on adjusting my own behavior, on doing whatever would be firmest and most respectful in the situation, I am able to *appear* in control, and pretty soon I begin to *feel* in control as well. In fact, most of the time the person I am dealing with changes his attitude because of my respectful and firm demeanor. But, again, that is not my primary concern. My chief concern is "How can I behave in a manner that I can be proud of, regardless of how irrationally this other person is acting?" Self-control is a powerful tool and the ideal-self exercise will help you define what it would take to exhibit self-control in any given situation.

Priorities

Just as important as knowing how your ideal self would respond to a situation is knowing when you have wasted too much time and energy on a problem. Sometimes the best thing to do with a problem person or situation is ignore it or move on, but without an objective standard it can be difficult to know when to do this. The priorities exercise can help you decide when to say, "Enough."

The theory behind this exercise is that matters of lesser importance in your life should not drain energy and time from the matters that are of greater importance. If they do, then your life is out of order and you begin to feel out of control. Sometimes we get caught up in fights about lesser things with people who are simply not that important to us, and we become locked into them, allowing them to steal time and energy away from our more important relationships. Let me give you a personal example.

I was once involved in a counselor chat group on the Internet. Initially, the idea appealed to me. It seemed like a good opportunity to network with other professionals and trade ideas about various cases, theories, and concerns. Sometimes, though, arguments would break out. I would easily become caught up in these arguments, especially if I had a stake in them. I can recall times when I would be sitting at the dinner table with my family, oblivious to everyone because I was mentally formulating an argument to use against some chat mate.

Once I realized that this activity, which I initially thought of as a pleasant diversion, was going to sap energy from the resources I saved for my wife and children, I knew that I had to set some limits with myself. The fact is that even though the topics were interesting to me, the arguments and the people really did not matter to my life enough to warrant such an expenditure of energy and time. Once I reminded myself of my own priorities and realized where that activity fit in relation to those priorities, I was able to comfortably pull back from the group. I remained a member of the group for a good while, but I never got as emotionally involved again, because I had a clear idea of how much energy I could spend on the group before I would start to withdraw from things that were more important to me. When I found myself getting caught up in a fight, I would firmly tell myself, "This just isn't worth it, Greg," and I could let it go.

Sometimes we need to give other people and relationships a similar priority check. It is easy to get caught up in, and even obsessed with, conflicts at the parish council, the neighborhood association, the PTA, and so on. Most of the time, such things are harmless diversions. But sometimes these things can really get under our skin. By having a clear idea of where particular people or activities fit into our priorities, we can determine how much energy and time we have to spend on them.

PRIORITIES: AN EXERCISE

Identify the ten most important activities and relationships in your life (spouse, work, God, kids, church, specific community activities). Write them down in any order.

Rank those people or activities from one to ten according to the priority they would ideally *hold in your life.*

Look at your list. Are the relationships and activities you ranked lower on your list negatively affecting the time and energy you give to conflicts occurring in relationships and activities you ranked higher on your list? If so, how will you set limits on those relationships and activities so that they stay "in their place"? If you are unable to set—and stick to—limits in a particular area of your life, this is probably a clear indication that you need to end your involvement in this relationship or activity. Not doing so will eventually tax your mental health and undermine the more important relationships in your life. The rule of thumb is get control over them or get out of them.

Think about other relationships and activities that are not on your list. Place these where you think they should ideally belong. Most will be below the ten most important things you already identified, but you might place some among those first entries.

Finally, consider these new items. Are the relationships and activities you ranked lower on your list negatively affecting the time and energy you give to conflicts occurring in the relationships and activities you ranked higher on your list? If so, how will you set limits on those relationships and activities? Get control over them or get out of them.

Throughout this chapter, I have tried to show you how to apply specific techniques to all the different relationships in your life so that you can discover the secrets of changing your world and keeping the change.

But regardless of the relationship or circumstance you find yourself in, remember that the most important question to ask is not "What can I do to change this person or my environment?" The most important question is actually a prayer. "Lord, what do you want me to learn about myself as a result of this problem relationship or circumstance? What are the strengths and virtues you are challenging *me* to develop?" If you can bring yourself to ask this question in the face of offensive people and adverse situations, you will not only grow in wisdom and strength, but it has been my personal and professional experience that God will give you the grace to resolve the problem as well. God is constantly testing and refining our hearts in the fires of adversity, but by seeking wisdom first, all things will become clear to us in the Lord's time, and Divine Peace will reign in our hearts and homes.

Epilogue

Nina, a woman who attended one of my seminars, recently called me to tell me her story. "I used to feel like such a doormat. I couldn't say no to anybody, and I always felt like I was being taken advantage of."

She had an especially hard time dealing with her family and her employers, who she experienced as unappreciative and demanding. "It seemed like the harder I tried to please everybody, the worse they treated me and the worse I felt."

Nina explained that many of the techniques I spoke of in my seminar, the techniques I have presented throughout this book, gave her a blueprint to follow and empowered her to take charge of her life and relationships. "I realized that we teach people how to treat us, and I was teaching people that it was okay to take advantage of me and not give me the appreciation I really deserved."

By applying the techniques presented in *God Help Me! These People Are Driving Me Nuts,* Nina was not only able to set better limits with people, but she was also able to stop resenting others for their slights. "I realized that it was silly to resent people for the things they did to me. After all, it wasn't as if they were really out to get me. For the most part, they just weren't thinking. Rather than resent them, I just had to do a better job of setting limits. Of teaching them how I wanted to be treated."

As Nina became better at teaching others how she wanted to be treated, she found that she experienced more peace in her life and more compassion for others. "I always thought of myself as a sensitive person. But I never realized how much anger I had inside of me. I used to resent so many people for the things they did that hurt me, mostly because I felt powerless to do anything about it. Now, I don't have that anger anymore. I realize that most people are just like me. We try our best, but sometimes we step in it, and when that happens, we need someone to tell us what we've done wrong and how not to do it again."

By practicing techniques such as seeing the positive intention behind the offensive behavior of others, using the P-E-A-C-E process, and setting respectful limits, Nina learned to see other people—even offensive people—as human beings who, like herself, sometimes made mistakes and required gentle correction. She was able, for the first time in her life, to make a meaningful, personal connection with two of the most important maxims of Christianity: Jesus' command to "Love your neighbor as you love yourself" and St. Augustine's teaching to "Love the sinner but hate the sin."

At the end of our conversation, Nina told me, "I don't have that anger anymore, and I don't feel like some kind of victim anymore either. I know I have a long way to go, but I feel so much more peaceful now. I feel like I have a better understanding of how to love others as Jesus wants me to, and I really feel him pouring out his grace on me so I can keep doing it."

That is my prayer for you, dear reader. That God would pour out his grace into your heart so that you can make the kinds of changes in your own life and attitudes that will empower you to love yourself in a healthy, Christian way and then love others as you love yourself.

While you can make peace with the difficult people in your life in many ways, I hope that the methods presented here have been helpful to you. And if there is any way I can be of additional assistance to you as you continue your spiritual and emotional journey toward discovering greater peace and love in your life, please do not hesitate to contact me at the Pastoral Solutions Institute, (740) 266-6461, or visit our Web site at www.CatholicCounselors.com.

I leave you with one prayer:

May God bless you and keep you.
May his face always shine upon you.
May God grant you pardon and peace all the days of your life.
(And may people stop driving you nuts.)
Amen.

Also by Gregory K. Popcak

Holy Sex!

A Catholic Guide to Toe-Curling, Mind-Blowing,Infallible Loving

Common wisdom portrays sex and church to be at odds, yet studies show that Catholics have better sex, and more often. This witty, frank, and refreshingly orthodox book draws from the beautiful truths of Catholic teaching to show people of all faiths about rich and satisfying sexuality. Hailed by Christians across the spectrum from Christopher West and Janet E. Smith to John L. Allen, Jr., *Holy Sex!* includes dozens of questionnaires, quizzes, and valuable lessons from real-life stories.

"This practical sex guide incorporates, but goes well beyond, marital sacramental theology, and as such will be welcomed by those who want to adhere to Catholic teaching yet still enjoy the passion of sexual union. He includes information on natural family planning (a Catholic Church–approved method of spacing births) and advice for sexual problems. His essential message makes this worthwhile reading."—*Publisher's Weekly*

978-0-8245-2471-5, paperback

A Marriage Made for Heaven

The Secrets of Heavenly Couplehood

Finally, a parish-based program for couples who are already married and wish to enrich their marriage. This 12-session marriage enrichment program helps couples apply rich theological content directly to their current married life. Instructing them with a variety of tools—including activities, DVD supplements, and group discussions—this resource shows spouses not only how to be closer with each other and their community but also how to fully enjoy the spiritual significance of their bond. As a trustworthy source that utilizes lessons from both the orthodox faith and the best research in marriage and family psychology the program is an ideal addition to any Catholic parish. Includes a leader guide (with 12-session DVD introduced by Bishop Conlon) and couples guide.

Leader Guide with DVD, 978-0-8245-2532-3, paperback

Couple Workbook, 978-0-8245-2533-0, paperback

God Help Me!

This Stress Driving Me Crazy!
Finding Balance Through God's Grace

The bills aren't paid, you didn't get enough sleep last night, and yesterday's work is only half-done. Whether at home or in the office, stress threatens to overwhelm everyone from time to time. How do you learn to control stress so that it doesn't control you? Using his years of experience as a Christian psychotherapist and host of the popular programs Fully Alive! and Heart Mind and Strength, Dr. Greg Popcak comes to the rescue with practical tips and tools for lessening anxiety. With religious insight and psychological wisdom —as well as a good dose of humor – he shows you how to avoid stress and maintain balance in life.

In this book, you'll discover:

- real-life stories and anecdotes showing how you can deal with stress
- checklists, quizzes, and questionnaires to help you identify your own situation
- clear explanations of the latest in psychological research on stress
- insights into how the sacraments enrich your life
- reminders of why God is more powerful than even your deepest trouble

978-0-8245-2598-9, paperback

About the Author

Dr. Gregory Popcak is one of the country's leading Christian counselors. Cohosting with his wife, Lisa Popcak, Greg brings his unique blend of Christian theology and counseling psychology nationwide with his daily radio call-in programs Fully Alive! (Catholic Channel–Sirius 159/XM1) and Heart Mind and Strength (Ave Maria Radio Network). Book readers also know Greg from his 8 bestselling books, including *Holy Sex!* and *A Marriage Made for Heaven*.

Greg's Pastoral Solutions Institute provides additional telephone counseling and other resources to Christians worldwide and is the largest organization of its kind in the world. If you are coping with marriage and family problems, depression and anxiety, sexual issues, problem habits, grief and loss, parenting questions, or ethical dilemmas, call today for more information on counseling, seminars, books, parish enrichment, and professional training.

The Pastoral Solutions Institute
234 St. Joseph Dr.
Steubenville, Ohio 43952
(740) 266-6461
www.CatholicCounselors.com